Guerrilla Music Marketing Handbook

Bob Baker

ISBN: 0-9714838-0-9

Published by Spotlight Publications, PO Box 43058, St. Louis, MO 63143 USA.

Table of Contents

TheBuzzFactor.com – Marketing ideas for songwriters, musicians and bands on a budget. Visit the site and sign up to get Bob's free music marketing tips by e-mail.

This Book Is Just One Part of an Ongoing Music Career Adventure

I hope your decision to read this book marks the beginning of a lengthy and successful journey. I'm confident that the principles and suggestions in this book will inspire you and help boost your self-promotion efforts to new levels. But the transaction shouldn't end there.

To make sure these ideas stick, I encourage you to visit my web site at **TheBuzzFactor.com**. There you'll find free articles and dozens of resources to help you get exposure, book more gigs, attract fans and sell more CDs.

While you're at the site, be sure to sign up for a free subscription to my e-mail newsletter, also called *The Buzz Factor*. The newsletter delivers a regular dose of music marketing tips and tools for songwriters, musicians and bands on a budget.

I'd love to hear from you, especially if you have a marketing tip or strategy you'd like to share with the nearly 10,000 music people who subscribe to *The Buzz Factor* newsletter.

Do yourself a favor and pay a visit to **TheBuzzFactor.com** the next time you're online. You'll be glad you did.

–Bob

Other books and resources by Bob Baker:

*What Every Musician Should Know About Self-Promotion:
The 29 Key Principles of Independent Music Marketing*

*Music Marketing Crash Course: 1,001 Ways to Promote Yourself,
Make Money and Live Your Dreams*

*Unleash the Artist Within: Four Weeks to Transforming Your Creative
Talents Into More Recognition, More Profit and More Fun*

*Branding Yourself Online: How to Use the Internet
to Become a Celebrity or Expert in Your Field*

*E-zine Music Marketing: Powerful Ways to Promote Your Music
with a Fan E-mail Newsletter*

Get more info at www.TheBuzzFactor.com

Introduction

Welcome to a new way of promoting your music. For decades, aspiring musicians thought the only legitimate route to success was landing a recording contract with a major record label. The times have definitely changed. The Internet and low-cost recording technologies have created a thriving do-it-yourself music movement. Unfortunately, thousands of songwriters and artists still believe the road to widespread recognition can only be traveled through a record deal.

I believe the best way to approach a career as a musician who writes and performs original music is to take control, get your hands dirty and market your music yourself. No one feels as strongly about your craft as you do. Which means you're the best person in the world to spread the news.

Sure, promoting your own music takes a lot of effort. But it's well worth it. And despite what you may have heard to the contrary, it can be profitable. Here are just a few examples of music people who have succeeded on their own terms:

- It took her more than four years and several hundred live shows to do it, but singer/songwriter April Nash (www.aprilnash.com) sold over 60,000 copies of her self-released CD.

- John Taglieri, a solo singer/songwriter from New Jersey (featured in Chapter 6), sold more than 4,000 of his own CDs primarily using the Internet.

- Working alone from his house in West Virginia, Scooter Scudieri (www.firstrockstar.com) sold 1,500 copies of his CD in six months, which led to an appearance on NPR's Mountain Stage radio show and an opening slot for Dave Matthews and NRBQ.

- Mikel Fair and his electronic music project 303infinity (www.303infinity.com) have earned nearly $250,000 through merchandise sales and performance royalties. Fair has a loyal fan base and a mailing list of thousands.

- Instead of shooting for a record deal, singer/songwriter Ellis Paul decided to concentrate on songwriting, getting in front of people and building a buzz. His first two independently released CDs sold more than 25,000 copies combined. Rounder/Philo Records later re-released one of his CDs.

Doing it yourself

You've most likely heard of singer/songwriter Ani DiFranco. Over a seven-year period she sold more than 400,000 copies of her many independent releases (an average of 66,600 units per year). In one year alone, DiFranco performed 130 shows and generated almost $2 million in gross ticket sales. She's been written about in glowing terms by just about every major magazine and newspaper in the country.

The astounding thing is, DiFranco accomplished all of this without a major record label, commercial radio airplay, MTV exposure or advertising. "If you are disgustingly sincere and terribly diligent, there are ways for any serious artist to operate outside the corporate structure," she once told the *Los Angeles Times*.

At age 20, DiFranco started her own label, Righteous Babe Records, and began performing a growing number of solo acoustic shows. Coffeehouse gigs led to colleges, then larger theaters and major folk festivals. DiFranco now has more than 30,000 people on her mailing list (with more signing on every show) and several employees who handle CD and merchandise orders from a warehouse in Buffalo, NY.

"My problem with the guys who run the music industry is that their only priority is to make money," she says. "My priority is to make music. The fact is, they need artists more than the artists need them."

So the next time you get down in the dumps because that major label recording contract hasn't come your way yet, pause and realize that – like DiFranco and other self-supporting musicians – you may be better off as an independent artist.

And don't think that the examples I use here are rare, isolated cases. Granted, most indie acts don't reach such impressive levels. But there are thousands of songwriters, musicians and bands turning a decent profit. And they're doing it on their own terms – doing something they have a real passion for: making and sharing music.

Putting your music career in focus

This manual was written to help you along the confusing path that leads to success with your music. The concepts, ideas and suggestions in these pages are simple. That's not to say they're always easy. There's work to be done here, but it's the kind of activity that's well within your ability to pull off.

The problem with most independent music people, even the ones who take lots of action, is that their energy is wasted on the wrong activities and unproductive methods. By the time you finish reading and working with this manual, you'll have a much clearer idea of how to direct your energies.

There are a couple of essential attitudes that run throughout this manual. They are:

1) **Whenever you take action to promote your music, you must know exactly what your purpose is and why you're taking the action to begin with.** The best way to make sure you're going about things effectively is to come up with a plan that makes sense, have very focused goals, and realize that you need to provide a benefit (or solution) to everyone you connect with in the music business.

2) **Think outside of your mental box.** Human beings are creatures of habit. We become victims of our own routines. Therefore, it's no surprise that we slip into a narrow way of doing things. Habits are quite useful when they involve brushing your teeth, getting dressed and driving a car. But when it comes to promoting your music, this routine way of thinking – and acting – is stunting your progress. When you market yourself the same way you've always done it, or the same way a thousand other artists have done it, you become part of the great indie music swamp in which everyone looks and sounds the same.

The guerrilla music marketing challenge

In this manual, I'll poke and prod you to be different, to expand your thinking, to focus your goals and actions – in essence, to become a true Guerrilla Music Marketer. We won't be talking about national advertising campaigns, music videos on MTV or worldwide distribution. Among other things, the following pages will show you how to:

- Work from the trenches, with little or no money.
- Use often-overlooked techniques to give your music wider exposure.
- Build a following one fan at a time.
- Use each small success as a stepping stone to a bigger and more significant success story.

I'm also going to ask you to do some serious soul searching and then commit your thoughts to paper by filling out the two Activity Worksheet sections. On these pages I've taken the main points covered throughout the manual and given you space to put your own responses. I implore you to use these worksheets! For it is here where my assorted suggestions come to life and become your own. By writing in these sections, you'll get a clearer idea of where you are and in what direction you need to be heading.

Guerrilla techniques in action

It was using these same guerrilla tactics while capturing my thoughts and goals on paper that led me to start playing music when I was 15 (the year was 1975, in case you're keeping score). In the 1980s I played the club circuit full time throughout the Midwest as a singer/guitarist/songwriter, and I later played in bands that each put out independent releases. I continue to play in a band part-time to this day.

I used many of the very ideas presented in this book to launch my own local music magazine in 1987. I didn't have much money to work with and had no connections or experience with publishing. What I did have was a good concept and a knack for writing. That newspaper, called *Spotlight*, grew and flourished for 10 years until I stopped publishing it in 1997. I put the paper to rest so I could concentrate on writing and marketing resources like this one.

In 1993, a company published my first book, *101 Ways to Make Money in the Music Business* (now out of print). Later that year I founded the St. Louis Regional Music Showcase, an annual music conference that ran for five years in the Midwest. In 1996, I self-published the first version of the book you hold in your hands.

In the late 1990s, I established an online presence as a resource for indie music marketing tips through my web site, TheBuzzFactor.com. At last count, my e-zine, also called *The Buzz Factor*, was approaching 10,000 subscribers. In more recent years, I've cranked out more books and spoken word audio CDs, including *What Every Musician Should Know About Self-Promotion*, *Music Marketing Crash Course*, *Unleash the Artist Within* and *Branding Yourself Online* – while also speaking at a number of music industry conferences.

Why the résumé listing? To make a point: I wasn't born into a wealthy family. I don't have friends who wield great power, nor do I have any special abilities. I'm certainly not a super salesman and I don't have a hyper, Type-A personality.

But I realized early on that I had a mind, just like everyone else's, that I could use to make great things happen. The only thing was, it seemed so many people around me felt as if they were victims of circumstance; that life handed them their fate and they were just along for the ride. That wasn't good enough for me. Through reading books and pondering about life for a while, I came to the conclusion that our lives are simply a reflection of our accumulated thoughts and actions. There's a great quote by Earl Nightingale that goes, "We become what we think about most of the time."

The secret to musical success

The problem with people living dead-end lives is that they think dead-end thoughts. People who enjoy successful lives think successful thoughts – and then follow those thoughts with positive action.

Once I realized this simple but powerful truth, I started directing my thoughts in more productive ways. And the actions followed quite naturally. No doubt, I've stumbled many times on my journey through life and the music business (and I continue to), but the rewards have been many. And they keep growing every year.

The Bottom Line: *Thoughts are things*. What starts as an intangible concept grows into a reality as a result of mental focus combined with real-life activity. In fact, this is exactly how all songs are created.

So I ask you: What thoughts do you have about your present and future as an independent music person? And what actions are materializing as a result?

The *Guerrilla Music Marketing Handbook* will help you sort out the answers, open your mind to the infinite possibilities around you and motivate you to take the steps necessary to climb higher up the ladder of success with your music.

How to use this book

Many of the chapters in this manual were originally written as separate special reports. While I have arranged them in a sequence that makes sense to me, you don't have to read the segments in any particular order. The same goes for the bonus special reports at the end of the manual.

However, I do suggest that you read Chapter 1, "The Power of Goal Setting: A Step-by-Step Plan for Reaching Your Musical Aspirations Faster," and Chapter 2, "The First 5 Steps to Marketing (and Profiting from) Your Music," first. These chapters give you a good foundation for the information contained in other chapters. Other than that, feel free to examine the chapters and reports that relate to whatever marketing or music career topic you want to focus on at the time.

Warning: While I've gone to great lengths to load up this book with creative marketing tactics and techniques, I encourage you not to get so consumed by the tactical details that you lose sight of the big picture: making great music and sharing it with a growing number of fans. It's not the web site, media exposure or CD cover art that's most important. What's most essential is how those things help you connect with more fans in a meaningful way.

I'm grateful that you're allowing me to share these ideas with you. I sincerely hope you soak up the tips revealed in these pages and put them to good use. I look forward to one day hearing about your far-reaching musical achievements.

Much success to you. Now get out there and promote yourself!

-Bob Baker

Chapter 1

The Power of Goal Setting: A Step-by-Step Plan for Reaching Your Musical Aspirations Faster

When the topic of goal setting comes up, most musicians run for cover. In fact, I'll bet that right now you're seriously thinking about skipping this chapter so you can move ahead to the "good stuff." That's understandable, but I urge you to ignore those instincts temporarily and stick with this page.

And while you're at it, relax. Planning for the future doesn't have to be painful. In fact, you'll find that getting on friendlier terms with the noble art of goal setting will propel you toward reaching your musical dreams – while also giving you more juice and energy with which to pursue them.

Of course, you may be one of those people who says, "Planning never gets me anywhere. I always run into brick walls and end up bitter and frustrated. No, I just like to let things happen and let nature take its course."

Warning: While there's nothing wrong with letting your instincts guide you toward your true passion in life, taking the "let-things-happen" approach too far often leads to bitterness and frustration.

How else can you explain the slew of cynical, wandering musicians who populate most music scenes? They muddle through gig after gig, waiting for nature to take its course, and then suddenly wake up one day and wonder why they're no better off today than they were five years ago.

The Ugly Truth: If you read nothing else in this chapter, at least contemplate this: When you just "let things happen" with your musical career, you take the steering wheel of success out of your hands. You'll always be at the mercy of someone or something else. In essence, you lose control over where you really want to take your skills and talents.

People who succeed in music use goal setting to get back in the driver's seat and step on that accelerator pedal known as "accomplishment." (Pardon the poetic car analogies, but they help make the point.)

The good news is that you most likely already possess the skills to set goals effectively. Have you ever written a song? Have you ever gone into a studio to record your music? If so, you've been setting goals and didn't even realize it.

Example: When you showed up at the studio for your first recording session, what did you do? Did you look at your fellow band members and say, "Jeez, I wonder what we should do now? Anybody got any good song ideas?"

Well, unfortunately, some musicians do this (I talk to studio engineers, you know), but hopefully you realize that not being prepared is senseless! You've got money invested in the session, you've had a dream to put out your own CD for years, plus you've got fans who are eagerly awaiting the recording ... you'd be nuts to go in there unprepared!

You didn't do that, did you?

Of course not. You went into that studio with a game plan – a list of songs, knowing who's playing what parts, when the harmonies come in, maybe even a title for the album. That's all that goal setting is: knowing what you want to do before you set out to do it.

So in the same way you'd be wasting your time and money not being prepared to go into that studio, so too are you wasting your precious resources by being unprepared when it comes to your overall career. Does that make sense to you?

Another Key Point: Goal setting is not a rigid science. The plans you come up with are fluid – you can expect them to evolve and change over time. This is yet another concept you should be familiar with, especially if you're a songwriter. Many songwriters (myself included) write using just a guitar or piano and voice.

However, when many of these artists create a new composition, they often hear much more than that sparse arrangement in their heads. The drums, the bass part, maybe an entire string section ... all of it is there in the mind's ear. Perhaps you create the same way.

Then you take this skeleton of a song and share it with your other band members, explaining to each the parts you hear ringing through your gray matter. But the song the band ends up playing and recording is usually quite different from the version you originally heard in your head. However, the newer version is almost always better.

Bottom Line: The plans you come up with when goal setting will change as you work toward them. But the mere act of coming up with an idea, visualizing it in your mind and acting on it will drive you to take those first important steps. While the end result isn't always the one you expected, it's usually one you can learn and grow from and hopefully be proud of.

By pushing yourself, through advance planning, to head off in a specific direction – whatever direction that is – you create the opportunities from which real success can be realized. By waiting for things to happen, though, you set the stage for stagnation. That's why setting goals for yourself and your music career are so important.

What follows are some helpful tips for getting the most out of goal setting:

Decide specifically what you want

Before you set out to conquer your goal, you have to know what you really want. Do you have a clear idea of what you're going after? Vague concepts about some day succeeding in the music business lead to vague, weak actions in attaining them.

However, detailed target goals – such as selling 3,000 units of your CD, playing 10 gigs a month, making at least $20,000 in the first quarter of next year – keep you focused and on track.

Visualize what you want as if you already have it

To be truly successful with goal setting, you must have a clear picture of the eventual outcome in your mind. Close your eyes and imagine what it would be like to reach the goal (or goals). Immerse yourself in that picture and deeply feel the sensations. What would it look, sound, feel, taste and smell like if you were already in that enviable position? Locking in these mental images will set you on an unstoppable course.

Write down your goals

Don't keep goals only in your head. Put ink to paper and commit them to a solid form. Writing down your goals adds another element of conviction to your intent to reach them. All of my accomplishments – publishing my music magazine, writing my books, putting out independent releases with my band – started as notes to myself jotted down in a notebook. Don't overlook the power of the pen.

In fact, I encourage you to take this a step further and set aside 20 to 30 minutes every day to write your goals and ideas in a notebook. Use these sessions to brainstorm new ways to promote your music, find solutions to current business problems or craft lyrics to an original song. Whatever you do, spend time writing – then apply the things you've written to reach your goals.

Make a list of what's in it for you

This is the fun part. Compile a list of ways you will benefit from achieving each goal. Will you be rewarded with recognition, self-fulfillment, money, fame or creative expression? By listing these benefits in detail, you examine your true motivation for wanting each goal in the first place. Sometime you may discover the reasons that drive you aren't the most productive (such as being lured by the prospect of making gobs of money, even though your heart isn't really into it).

However, when you have a goal that's fueled by a genuine desire and true belief in your ability to attain it and enjoy the benefits, you'll be energized and ready to take on the challenges.

Anticipate the obstacles you'll encounter

Make no mistake about it, there will be bumps along the road to reaching your goals. You will encounter things that go wrong, people who disappoint you, schedules that move slower than you'd like ... but don't let any of these obstacles stop you! Just try to anticipate some of the difficulties you'll face, then imagine and plan for how effectively you'll deal with them when they arise.

For five years, I organized an annual music conference in the Midwest called the St. Louis Regional Music Showcase. It was an enormous undertaking, and every year I had to gather a team of volunteer organizers who helped pull off the event. Without fail, every year one of my assigned organizers bailed out close to the event, leaving that aspect of the conference in disarray.

It was frustrating, but it seemed to be the nature of the beast. Instead of getting too upset about it, I either found a replacement or ended up doing the job myself (not always an attractive option). But since I had mentally prepared myself for this possibility, I was able to find a way to work through it. Plan on doing the same thing along the road to reaching your goals.

Identify the people and resources that can help you achieve your goals

Start gathering information on the people, tools and information sources you may need to reach your goals faster. These will include nightclubs, web sites, recording studios, music sales outlets, conferences, booking agents, radio stations, magazines, graphic designers, producers, etc.

Compile this list of contacts from music business directories and by networking with other musicians. Plus, you should always keep your eye open for new sources to add to the list – newspapers you pick up in other cities, music associations you read about, new resources you come across on the Internet, etc.

You can't do it completely on your own – remember, it's a business of people ... and timely information.

Here's a short list of valuable directories and web sites you should look into:

Musician's Atlas
www.musiciansatlas.com
A 350-page guide that offers more than 15,000 music business contacts in over 25 categories, including press, booking agents, managers and record labels. Listings include current names, phone and fax numbers, e-mail and web site addresses, detailed submission policies and the styles of music preferred.

Recording Industry Sourcebook
www.isourcebook.com
For the industry professional, the *Sourcebook* is an ideal desktop reference. For the artist, it is a tool to access the music industry – from where to record and rent pro audio equipment to selecting a designer for your album cover and producing your music video. Contains more than 12,000 listings in about 60 categories.

Radio-Locator
www.radio-locator.com
A comprehensive radio station search engine with links to over 10,000 web pages and audio streams from radio stations around the world.

News Directory
www.newsdirectory.com
More than 15,000 links to newspaper and magazine web sites.

NewsLink
www.newslink.org
A great directory of newspapers, radio broadcasters and TV stations.

Independent Record Store Directory
www.the-ird.com/store.html
Here you'll find the best places to sell music across the United States.

Record Labels on the Web
www.rlabels.com
A web site filled with 5,000-plus links to record label web pages.

Set a deadline

Remember how you always got off your butt and went to work the night before a term paper was due? Deadlines have a way of motivating us to act. So do commitments we make to others and ourselves. Set a time limit for achieving each stage of your goal-setting action plan ... then do whatever it takes to meet those deadlines.

Make sure your deadlines are realistic. If they're set too far in the future, there may be no motivation for you to get busy working toward them. If deadlines are set too soon, you risk encountering disappointment if you run out of time and miss them. Do your best to set sensible goals.

Create your plan

After you've taken all the previous steps, it's time to write the first draft of your action plan. To do this, start with the goal itself and work backwards through the process. Keep breaking every stage of the plan down into its most basic tasks (such as making phone calls, mailing packages, booking studio time, setting up meetings, writing songs).

Then make a short list of the primary things that need to be done first – but make sure they're basic, attainable steps. For instance, if your goal is to sell 50,000 copies of your self-released CD, calling a major distributor would not be the first thing you'd do. There is a whole series of preliminary steps you'd need to take long before you ever got near a distributor.

Now get to work and write that first-draft plan!

Clear your mind, then re-examine and refine your plan

This is one of the few times I'll suggest you not take immediate action. Get away from your action plan for about a day or so and let the details float around in your subconscious mind while you work on other things.

After some time away, come back to the plan with a fresh eye and start evaluating the logic in your sequence of events. For instance, have you really allowed enough time for the recording of your demo? Or perhaps you're being too easy on yourself by allowing six months to get your first band photo taken. (I've known bands that have been together for years and have never had a promotional photo taken. In fact, I think I was in one.)

Are you juggling too many or too few projects at the same time? Also ask yourself what additional help you might need with technical support, media contacts, artwork, web design, press releases and more.

Next, create your second-draft plan as best you can. But remember, it doesn't have to be perfect to use. Don't fool yourself into thinking you can't get started just because there are a few details you don't know yet. Trust your abilities and know you'll handle whatever needs to be done when demanding situations arise.

Act on your goals now!

At some point you must get busy working on the plan you've just created. It's sad, but a lot of great ideas have withered away because the person who came up with them never took action. Don't let this be your fate. Don't wait for nature to takes its mystical course.

Vow that every day you will take some action based on your goal-setting plan. Even if you think you don't have time or aren't feeling motivated, do at least some small deed every single day. Even if it's simply making one phone call to a media contact, writing one letter to an entertainment lawyer, sending one e-mail message to a club owner, responding to one fan letter ... do something every day!

Measure your progress and make adjustments

Once you come up with a plan and start working on it every day for a couple of months, you must then determine if your actions are leading you in the right direction. Are you moving closer to your goal or further away? Is your progress happening slower or faster than you hoped?

The only way to answer those questions is to regularly evaluate your plan and measure your progress. If you find that you're way behind schedule on getting things done, ask yourself what you can do to get the results you really want. Don't just get frustrated and give up. Making adjustments to your plan is an essential part of any goal-setting process. So be prepared to measure often and come up with solutions.

When something is working, fit more of it into the plan. When other aspects prove to be duds (like the drummer's bright idea to send your guitar player to local radio stations dressed like Barney the dinosaur), cut back or drop them completely. Fine-tuning is what working your goal-setting plan is all about.

Put the art and craft of goal setting to work to focus your energy and give you an immense boost toward getting what you really want from your music – and from your life!

Chapter 2

The First Five Steps to Marketing (and Profiting From) Your Music

To borrow a phrase from former President Clinton, "I feel your pain."

I'm not talking about physical pain, of course. I'm referring to the deep emotional pain and stress that come with pouring your heart into your band, new CD or other music-related pursuit ... and still feeling like you're coming up short.

Whether you produce pop, rock, jazz or ethnic music, you know what you offer is good and is of value to others. It's just that not enough people seem to know about you yet and, as a result, not nearly enough money is streaming in to cover expenses and give yourself a little take-home money.

Take heed, my fellow Guerrilla Music Marketer. This chapter sheds light on how to remedy your situation (without losing your sanity or forcing you to start a Vanilla Ice tribute band). What follows are five steps you must follow to take charge of your music marketing so you start profiting from it *now*!

Warning: Don't make the mistake that many aspiring music biz wannabes make. They read these steps, tell themselves how valuable the advice is, and then go back to the same destructive routines as before. You won't do that.

And to make sure you don't, I've added an affirming commitment statement to the end of each step. Read them out loud every day for at least two or three weeks until the commitment becomes ingrained. Then read them at least once a week after that. Doing so will make certain you put these success tips into action ... and profit accordingly.

1) Have a clear idea who your ideal fan is

Could you sit down right now and write a profile of your ideal fan? Can you articulate how your fans dress, where they work, what TV shows they watch, what they do for fun, and who their favorite cultural hero is?

If you can't describe your fans in detail, you should immediately start searching for a way to do so. Knowing precisely who your fans are dictates what avenues you use to reach them and how you communicate your message once you do reach them.

Reality: Continuing to ignore these insights will lead to missed opportunities and wasted resources. If you don't know where your fans hang out, what they're interested in, and why they spend money, how will you ever be able to effectively promote your talents in a way that will lead to all of you being better off?

When you overlook this element, potential fans move on without the benefit of your music. And you stumble on without the satisfaction of having shared your music and getting the recognition and income that come with it.

The Solution: Do some basic, informal research. If you perform live at all, start asking questions of people in the crowd during breaks and after your shows. Write down your observations. What types of people come to see you? What traits do your fans have in common? Asking questions may even allow you to discover a segment of the population you've been ignoring, but which could benefit from your music.

If you're just starting out, observe the types of people who patronize similar artists. Or simply describe the type of person to whom you want your band or record label to appeal. This doesn't have to be a complicated research project. Just get a handle on the types of people you want to reach with your promotional and sales messages. Doing so will help you get to them faster.

Affirm your commitment to step 1:

"I no longer leave my music marketing to chance. Through basic research, personal observation and gut instincts, I create a specific profile of my ideal fan. Using this profile, I know how to reach my fans and communicate with them effectively."

2) Discover what motivates your fans to spend time and money on you

Now that you have a clearer idea of who your fans are, you have to reach out and touch them. But the only way to reach them effectively is to understand their real reasons for spending time and money on you.

The Problem: Most music marketers concentrate on themselves and the features of their product or service. For instance, recording studios are notorious for promoting lists of equipment and the credentials of engineers. That's not a crime, but the real reasons many studio clients spend money is to get the good feeling of hearing a major label-quality recording of their music (because of the equipment) and getting respect for being so closely connected to the music industry (due to the engineer's resume).

While the studio literature and sales pitch should be stressing the clients' feelings of accomplishment and respect, they instead spit out a list of mechanical features. The trick is to push a consumer's hot buttons – the deeper reasons he/she spends time and hard-earned money on a given product or service.

Paul and Sarah Edwards, authors of the book *Getting Business to Come to You*, remind us that all potential buyers are tuned into radio station WII-FM, which stands for "What's In It For Me?" – the essential question that every person asks when confronted with a time or money decision.

"Clients want to know that what you provide will meet their needs," the authors write. "Can you save your customers money, time or effort? Can you increase their ability to compete? Can you make them look good to others? Can you give them peace of mind? Put yourself in the customer's shoes."

Bottom Line: Determine the real motivating feeling – the key benefit – that people experience when they spend time and money on you. Does your music make them feel good? Does it give them a recreational escape from their worries? Does it allow them to hang onto something they're afraid of losing, such as youth, sex appeal or an outlet for their frustrations?

Ask your fans more questions, make more observations, do your homework and use your head. Discovering the key motivations that draw your fans to you will help you discover your road to success in the music business.

Affirm your commitment to step 2:

"Just knowing who my fans are is not enough. I now do whatever it takes to uncover the personal and emotional benefits that motivate people to spend time and money on my music. Discovering these hot buttons allows me to more effectively market the music I have to offer."

3) Create and use a Brand Identity Statement (BIS)

Think of your band or music business as the steel tip of a dart. Now visualize that the people of the world are spread out across a giant wall filled with thousands of dartboards. Each dartboard represents a specific demographic group. For instance, one might be teenagers who like hard rock music while another symbolizes adults who enjoy the blues. Other dartboards might include fans of folk, country, acid jazz, punk, R&B and so on.

Key: When you market your music, it's your job to aim the tip of your dart directly at the bull's-eye of the dartboards that represent your ideal fans. You do this by sending targeted messages to the newspapers, magazines, radio stations, web sites and mailing lists used by potential fans.

That's the whole point of all this soul-searching research. Once you know who you're ideal fans are, you can determine what forms of media they patronize. Then send focused messages through those channels.

But what kind of messages do you send? Most people who market independent music make one of two mistakes. They either:

1) Throw their dart randomly all over the wall and accomplish little or nothing, or

2) Aim their dart at the proper boards, but the message is so weak, the dart doesn't stick to any of them.

The Solution: Create a Brand Identity Statement (BIS) about your music. A BIS is a simple but powerful sentence of no more than 15 words (10 words or less is even better) that describes the specific vision of your songs, image, band or record label. If you could take every feature and beneficial aspect associated with your music and run them through a grinder, only to be left with the pure, concentrated essence of you and your music ... that would be your BIS.

You should craft your BIS to include a benefit statement to your fans. Two well-known BISs from the traditional business world are Domino's "Fresh, hot pizza delivered to your door in 30 minutes or less, guaranteed" (13 words) and M&M's "Melts in your mouth, not in your hands" (eight words).

The BIS I use to promote free e-mail subscriptions to my Buzz Factor newsletter is "Free marketing ideas for songwriters, musicians and bands on a budget." As for the music newspaper I used to publish, the BIS I used to lure potential advertisers was "Your direct link to St. Louis music/entertainment consumers."

Examples: Here are a few possible Brand Identity Statements for bands:

- "Old-school funk for people who like to dance"
- "Upbeat power pop: If you're sick of dark, brooding grunge bands, you need us"
- "Erotic techno grooves for sensuous souls"

Other BISs might include the following:

- A recording studio could use "High-quality demos for bands on a budget."
- A solo artist targeting bar owners might use "Riveting acoustic folk music to help you sell more beer."

- A small ticket agency's BIS could be "Convenient access to the great shows the big promoters miss."

You can use your Brand Identity Statement in two ways. One is internal; the other external.

Internal – Having a BIS keeps you focused on your marketing message. Therefore, every time you write a news release, set up a photo session, do a radio interview or design an album cover, you make certain your vision stays focused on your core identity. You wouldn't want your album cover to convey humor while the faces in your band photo look grim and serious.

Also, using a BIS keeps your marketing message tight and consistent. You don't want to send out a news release about your band's new online resource for ska fans, then do a radio interview and end up talking only about the night you met Pat Sajak. By constantly referring to your BIS, you make sure the messages you send stay focused on the most potent aspects of your music.

External – You can also use your BIS as a musical slogan that appears on all of your ads, fliers, news releases, banners, posters, T-shirts, stickers and more. That way, whenever people hear your name, they will be reminded of your musical identity and what's in it for them.

Here are some real-life examples of Brand Identity Statements in use:

- Canada's Helios Design and Communications uses "Hard-hitting design, done right the first time."
- H&B catalog of Jazz CDs claims to be "A mail order service for people who know jazz."
- Chicago's Smart Studios promotes itself with the BIS "Great sounds. Cool people. Killer studio."
- The band Buck O Nine describes its music as "Rock-steady ska-core from southern California."

Find your own BIS. Then use it to stay focused and hammer home your primary marketing message to the masses.

Affirm your commitment to step 3:

"I will never again 'wing it' when it comes to marketing my music. I now use a powerful Brand Identity Statement to promote my music. I use my BIS to develop a consistent, needle-sharp vision and focused public image of my unique niche in the world of music."

4) Focus on the benefits of your music – not the features

Now it's time to connect with the music fans whose lives you are about to improve. But first we're going to dissect the way you communicate with these fans. We'll start by using the information you gathered about who your fans are and why they spend time and money on you. Then you'll use those details as you pursue various means of communicating your message, including:

- News releases sent to the media
- Your brochure, letterhead and business card
- Your promo package and photos
- Paid ads
- E-mail messages
- Web pages
- Fax messages
- Voice mail
- Posters
- Radio interviews
- Album cover artwork
- Direct mail pieces

Bottom Line: As you create the marketing materials listed above, you must keep one thing foremost in your mind: the needs of your fans! In other words, stop talking so much about yourself, your needs and your qualifications. Start talking about what matters most: The benefits fans get when they support your music.

"The objective here is plain," says marketing expert Jeffrey Lant. "It is not merely to tell what you've got ... it's to motivate a human being to take immediate action so you can move to the next stage of the marketing process." Lant has self-published over ten business books (including *Cash Copy* and *Money-Making Marketing*) and has sold a ton of them using the same tactics he preaches about in them.

In his book *No More Cold Calls*, Lant advises, "You must list every feature of your service, transform every one into a benefit, then make sure the benefit is as specific and enticing as possible."

Let's see how this works in the real world. As an example, I'll use the way I've marketed my spoken-word audio books. I'll list each feature first, then its corresponding benefit.

Feature: Sixty minutes in length.

Benefit: Jammed packed with a full hour of career-boosting details you can start using the same day you receive them.

Feature: Available only in audio format.

Benefit: Soak up these useful success secrets at your convenience: while you drive, jog, ride a bike or clean the house. Audio books make learning easy.

Feature: Order securely online now.

Benefit: Why wait? Start putting these ideas to use sooner by taking advantage of this safe and convenient ordering option. You'll have the recording in five to seven days if you place your order online now.

Get the idea?

Affirm your commitment to step 4:

"No more bland résumé listings for me! I now take every feature related to myself and my music and transform them into benefits that my clearly defined audience of potential fans find irresistible."

5) Stop talking so much about yourself

I know it seems like we've beaten this premise to death. But just in case it hasn't sunk in, let's drive it home one more time: Make certain your words – whether in person or on the phone, by e-mail or on your web site, in ads or sales letters – focus on the benefits to your fans.

Time and time again I explained this essential concept to some of the business owners who advertised in my former music newspaper. And, sure enough, when they turned in the wording for their ads, they were filled with "I can do this, we've done that, I, me, mine ... blah, blah, blah!"

Reality: Human beings gravitate toward talking and thinking about themselves. And for a good reason. For millions of years, members of our species had to think about their own needs to survive. In the caveman days, if you weren't consumed with self-preservation, you'd be consumed by any number of wild predators, not to mention being done in by members of rival tribes. There's a long-standing tradition of human self-indulgence.

So you're not going to wipe out millions of years of conditioning in a couple days. But you can use your advanced, reasoning brain to resist these primitive urges when it comes to marketing your music-related pursuits.

Also, realize that you can use this knowledge of human nature to your advantage. When you approach potential fans through your live shows, web site, business cards, mailing pieces and so on, who are they focused on? Don't kid yourself and think it's you.

Knowing this, give fans what they want and make sure your marketing message hits them squarely on the head with what's in it for them. Lead off with the number one benefit fans get from you, followed by the number two benefit and so on. Pile the motivating reasons they should care about you one on top of the other until even the most thickheaded of humans can figure it out.

A more specific example: Let's say you were put in charge of marketing a new electric drill for carpenters. How would you go about it? Most people would start listing features: the manufacturer, mechanical specs and material the drill is made of ... all focusing on – you guessed it – the drill. But what do people really want when they buy a drill?

A hole.

They also want a hole that can be created quickly, easily and economically. It really doesn't matter if the hole gets there because of a drill, a toaster, a pair of socks or a monk – as long as the appropriate hole is conveniently creating in the appropriate place.

In other words, sell the hole, not the drill. Then, and only then, use your features to show how your drill can meet the customer's specific needs.

Affirm your commitment to step 5:

"It isn't all about me. I resist the human urge to talk about myself and will, instead, focus on what my fans are most interested in: what's in it for them!"

There you have it: The first five steps to more effective music marketing. Now affirm your commitment to these principles and get busy thinking, observing, asking questions, researching your ideal fans, creating a BIS, focusing on the benefits you offer and more. A world of notoriety and profit awaits you.

Chapter 3

35 Ways to Promote Yourself, Your Band or Your New Release

Despite what you may have heard to the contrary, promoting and marketing your music shouldn't be the dreary task so many music people make it out to be. The pessimists tell us we have to shut down the creative side of our brains and shift into "business" mode. How dull. How boring. No wonder so many folks go running for the hills at the mere mention of having to promote their music.

What follows is a list of creative, low-cost ideas and techniques you can start using right away to market your music. Read these tips. Think about them. Play with them. Have some fun with them. But, most importantly, put them into action … starting today!

Translate your story into something that's newsworthy

Announcing the release of another new album won't get you very far. Music magazines get dozens of these ho-hum announcements every day. However, the debut release from an Iraq War veteran or a guy who once got punched by Sean Penn might catch the attention of a music editor. Why? Because it has a news hook that makes it stand out.

So what's your news hook? Does your band name or new CD title have a significant meaning? Have any of your members won awards, done brave deeds or accomplished anything noteworthy (they don't have to be music-related)? Do the lyrics to any of your songs tie in with a current event or trend? Always be on the lookout for fresh news hooks related to your music and then hammer them home to the media.

Here's a sampling of free press that artists have received in various publications over the years – along with the news hooks they used to get it:

1) The east coast band Too Much Joy received a letter from former Speaker of the House Newt Gingrich letting the members know that the group's tune "Theme Song" had inspired countless Republican activists to pursue their conservative agenda during a recent election.

The only thing was, members of Too Much Joy never supported Gingrich and didn't consider themselves to be politically right leaning in any way. The *Aquarian Weekly* plastered its cover with the news item and filled up two full pages inside dealing with the issue.

Have you received a letter from a public figure? Could you write to someone well-known and request that they write a brief note about your music? ***Another option:*** When a famous author comes to your town for a book signing ... buy the book, get in line and ask him or her to write a special inscription – such as "The Lipsmackers Rock! -Dr. Phil." Make photocopies of the signature and leverage it to get as many plugs in the media as you can.

2) The Texas-based band Rare Seed got a blurb in a local paper regarding its upcoming appearance on a regional music video program. This is a smart ploy. Most music people celebrate when they get the media to cover them. And then stop. These band members, on the other hand, used their success with television to lure the print media into also giving them a plug.

Why not use this cross-media technique with radio and Internet media sources, too? Use every achievement as a stepping stone to your next marketing move. If done right, it's a never-ending process.

3) Dr. Frank, who fronts the Bay area band Mr. T Experience, received some press in *Bam* magazine regarding the "Dr." part of his stage name. It seems Frank was all set to attend graduate school at Harvard when he changed course to form a punk band instead.

Do you have an alternate career path you've either put on hold or are doing as a day job? If so, how can you squeeze some media exposure out of it? If the usual music papers and columnists don't nibble, what about trade publications or company newsletters associated with your other line of work?

4) The members of 1,000 Mona Lisas garnered a write-up concerning an incident that had them pulled over in Texas with state troopers searching them and their van for drugs. The band also happened to call its next tour "Got Any Weed?" Now it's your turn ... not to get pulled over, but to take a frustrating situation and turn it into a promotional device.

What awful things have happened to you lately? And how can you turn them into a newsworthy advantage for you and your music?

5) Twelve San Francisco bands got press when they pooled their efforts and produced a calendar. Each month featured a photo of a different act with humorous events that happened to each band on various dates. Could you use this angle for your band?

6) The band Her Majesty the Baby got a blurb written because it was the first band on its indie label to release an album on a new, enhanced CD format. Do you have a unique way of presenting yourself?

7) One hard-core Beatles fan got exposure when he persuaded the mayor of his city to declare December 8 as "John Lennon/Free as a Bird Day." Could you swing a similar proclamation?

8) WVRV radio in St. Louis gets exposure every year when it hosts its annual holiday "River of Toys" benefit concert, featuring national and regional artists performing in an acoustic setting. What worthy cause could you support?

9) Silverwolf Records got coverage for its *Homeless Project*, a compilation CD of songs about the homeless. Does your CD have a noteworthy theme?

10) A rap trio whose members pack on a few extra pounds performed a promotional workout at a New York fitness club. The media gathered and got photos and video of the rappers sweating to the sounds of their new single.

Now come up with your own news hooks. And remember, have fun doing it!

Blurbs, short takes and mentions equal good exposure for you

Some people call them "blurbs." Others call them "short takes" or "brief editorial mentions." Whatever name you give them, they can add up to extra media exposure for you and your music. Feature stories and record reviews are great – and you should pursue these avenues of media coverage regularly. But what most music marketers overlook are the great opportunities that exist with music gossip columns, scene reports, industry updates, studio news and more.

Every week, thousands of magazines, newspapers, web sites and fanzines around the world need to fill certain editorial sections with short, music-related items of interest. Since they're not especially prominent, these sections are ignored by bands and record labels. How foolish.

What follows is a list of column blurbs I found while flipping through a few regional music papers. Use these ideas to come up with your own list of angles to get regular editorial mentions.

11) The nostalgic R&B group the Fabulous Boogie Kings received some positive press after a club appearance in Houston. The blurb made a reference to the outstanding sales of the band's latest CD. Do you have something of note to celebrate – an achievement that lends credence to your band's worth? If so, share it with the press.

12) Personality Crisis received a media mention because the band was planning a special show to celebrate its 500th gig. Any special occasion – no matter how trivial it may seem to you – can be leveraged into a reason for a columnist to give you a plug.

13) A few Texas bands put together a rock show package called the Divas of Rock Tour. Combining your efforts with other bands, record labels or a group of sponsors – and adding a theme – opens the door to more exposure.

14) Shaun Barusch got a few great media plugs when he formed MIA Records. Artists aren't the only subjects to get mentioned in the press. Consider your label, distribution company, charity, studio – whatever – as a prime candidate for coverage.

Here are more real-life editorial blurbs:

15) Hard rock band Third Eye got written up after making an appearance at the Milwaukee Metal Festival.

16) Arts organization the Houston Music Council got press when it released the 4th volume of a compilation CD featuring local bands.

17) The publication *Music News* ran a blurb on the Zealots' performance at a regional street festival. The short piece also included the band's telephone hotline number.

18) The group Deadhorse received a write-up regarding its new guitarist.

Now start thinking. Start writing down your ideas. Start getting exposure!

More creative music marketing ideas

19) Canadian entertainment lawyer Ryan Richardson works with a band called Leaderdogs for the Blind, which released an album called *Lemonade*. Richardson says that when the record company that put out the CD did little to promote it, the band members decided to push their own singles – one being the title track, "Lemonade."

"Inserted with a flier listing the singles was a small packet of brand-name lemonade drink mix that cost us a whopping five cents each," he says.

"Because the packages were so compact, there was no additional cost to mail them. Across the country, radio program directors and DJs apparently fought over who was going to keep the tasty beverage, and the singles ended up charting." For most bands, this creative marketing ploy would have been enough. But not for the Leaderdogs.

Richardson explains, "At one of our summer festival shows, we distributed free homemade lemonade to the audience in 95-degree weather, as well as chilled cartons of the refreshment that had been donated by a local juice bottler for all of the industry types present. It worked well to reinforce the name of the song."

20) The Costa Mesa, CA band Saint Monday set up an in-store appearance at a Virgin Megastore location and gave away hundreds of free cassette samplers in five hours. Each sampler tape had a coupon for a $2 mail-in rebate that customers could get if they came back and bought the band's full-length CD at the store.

Since Saint Monday is promoting pop music with a fun and sexy image, the members are considering another creative tactic: giving away condoms with an inscription that reads "Saint Monday: Music That Turns You On."

So what are you doing that's fresh and different to promote yourself as an artist? Not sure what creative marketing strategy to try next? Try this:

21) Sit down right now with a pen and notebook. Start brainstorming on every possible angle for a creative hook. Consider the name of your band, the title of your new CD, maybe even the subject matter of individual songs. Also think about current events and good causes you feel strongly about.

Ask yourself: "How can I take these details about my music and transform them into a newsworthy and attention-getting story?" Write down your answers. You might be surprised by the great ideas you uncover.

Combine your clout with others and create your own music events

You know the philosophy by now: *Don't wait around for music marketing opportunities to come to you. Instead, create your destiny by taking matters into your own hands.*

Nowhere is this more powerful than with music events you conceive and organize with other people. To illustrate the point, here are some possible avenues to pursue:

22) Throw a listening party. Get together a group of bands and artists who have put out new CDs recently. Find a nightclub or record store that's supportive of local music. Then ask for a date to hold a new music listening party.

On the night of the listening party, pick someone to emcee (maybe you) and introduce one act at a time, then play one or two tracks off each band's CD. At the end of each group's segment, you could have people in the audience ask the players questions.

You could also offer free (or cheap) food and drinks and discounted prices to anyone who wanted to buy any of the CDs that night. It would be best to promote this as a safe, quick musical buffet for consumers who want to sample local music without having to hop from one beer-soaked club to another.

I wish more bands used this concept.

23) Present a collaborative, multi-act unplugged show. Sure, you could present an acoustic performance with other musicians at a nightclub or record store. The format works … but a lot of artists have done the same thing. It would be more interesting to take an extra step and stage an acoustic show at an unexpected venue. *Possibilities:* art galleries, skate shops, hip clothing stores, recreation centers, shopping malls, new age retailers, book stores, etc.

Once again, get a number of other acoustic acts on the bill and make sure the manager of the location is committed to actively promoting the event. Come up with a newsworthy theme and – combined with the offbeat location – you might have a nice angle with which to lure the media into covering it.

24) Tie into an already existing event. You don't have to reinvent the wheel to cash in on events. You can also contact the organizers of already established events and ask if you could help them add a musical element. That way, they look good and you get exposure. Think about the many annual events in your region. Which ones would benefit from your talents and creativity?

Hot tip: If you can't formally get connected to an existing event, consider presenting an unofficial party at a nearby location. Many artists and labels do this during major music conferences such as South by Southwest.

Sneak into media exposure through the side door

25) New age artist Laurie Z was interviewed once on a syndicated radio show called *Tech Talk* (which is also broadcast on the Internet). The program features people who use modern technology in various fields. Past guests have included Tom Clancy, Kurt Russell and Todd Rungren. Laurie was invited to discuss how she's used technology to create her music and market herself.

The main thing to note in this example is that a musical act is getting media exposure on a non-music show – a valuable lesson for us all. How many potential avenues of promotion are you overlooking because you don't see an immediate connection between what various media cover and what you produce?

Here are some possible angles for different genres:

26) A musician could hook up with a psychologist or music therapist to discuss the stress-reduction benefits of mellow jazz music.

27) A traditional blues player who has either lived through or learned a lot about regional music history could pitch himself as an expert on local culture.

28) A punk or metal band member could become an advocate for safe mosh-pit etiquette and offer to enlighten kids and their parents on common-sense advice when attending concerts.

29) A rap artist might shed light on the fact that not all rap and hip-hop music is about gangs, sex and life on the streets.

30) A country musician could team up with a fitness instructor and espouse the virtues of line dancing as a fun form of exercise.

31) Become a music trivia expert. Do you know way too much about the Beatles? Or Elvis? Or the '50s, '60s or '70s? Or some other musical niche? If so, appoint yourself to be your area's media consultant on the topic.

Bottom line: You no doubt have many media exposure angles you have yet to use to your advantage. Now is the time to discover them and put them to use!

Still more music marketing tips to consider:

32) Keep in touch with your contacts. Make sure that at least every six weeks your fans and industry contacts get a phone call, post card, e-mail or other new offering from you. Are you staying in touch with these people now? Your goal should be to regularly put your name and musical identity into the minds of the people who are in a position to support you. ***Tip:*** Come up with a schedule that would accomplish more frequent contact with the people who matter most to your career.

33) Keep your ears open for ideas. Listen to the music-related things people complain about, and then provide a solution to their problem. For instance, members of the Chicago band Cool Beans heard music fans complaining about all the negative, angst-ridden lyrics in modern rock songs. Since they play upbeat alternative pop, they started using the phrase "Energetic new rock & roll ... without the angst!" on all their fliers. Doing so positions them as the "alternative" to gloom rock. And they might not have used that approach if they hadn't listened to what people were saying.

34) Spell out your music for potential new customers. New age artist John Huling puts a brief description of his music on the back of his CDs. By doing so, even customers who haven't heard his music before can get a quick synopsis of his style and what musical benefits he offers.

Lesson: Don't expect people to automatically know what your music is all about. There is nothing wrong with indie artists putting review quotes and testimonials from happy fans on the back of CD sleeves. Just be picky about which ones you use, focusing more on the quotes that spell out the heart of your musical message and the hard-hitting benefits listeners get when they hear it.

35) Make a commitment to do something every day to promote your music. If a day goes by that you don't do at least some small act to promote your music, you're cheating yourself. And the promotional action you take doesn't have to be earth-shattering. Simple actions are effective, too – as long as they're done regularly.

Ultimate success in music comes as a result of the small steps you take consistently on a daily basis. Pick something covered in this chapter every day and put it to use. Doing so will earn you more fans, more notoriety and more clout ... for weeks, months and years to come!

Chapter 4

How to Exploit the Music Media and Get the Widespread Exposure You Deserve

It's a sad fact, but most independent songwriters, musicians and bands never get around to pursuing the big-time media coverage they talk so much about. Sure, they say they're serious about getting exposure through hundreds of college and alternative radio stations, music magazines, newspapers, web sites and e-zines. I hear the same thing from people who are supposedly marketing a music-related product or service.

These music people appear to be sincere about garnering the profitable exposure and attention that comes with a well-executed media assault. The idea of program directors, editors and writers calling to get an artist's latest CD or promo package seems to genuinely turn these people on.

Reality: Guess what? These same people talk so much they forget one important thing: *Actually putting their words into action and making the media exposure dream become a reality!*

So after a while these artists stop talking and simply get comfortable living in the obscurity of what I call "Media Limbo." Which means thousands of music fans never hear about the great musical stuff they have to offer.

DON'T MAKE THIS SAME MISTAKE!

There are ways of getting the widespread media exposure you need. But first you have to leap over a few hurdles that are currently keeping you from getting to that enviable position.

Before we address those topics, I must point out that this chapter does not cover *who* to contact. There are many excellent music industry directories available to help you gather names and addresses. In addition to the resources listed in Chapter 1, you may also want to hunt down the *Musician's Guide to Touring and*

Promotion (www.musiciansguide.com, 800-745-8922) or my e-book, *The Online Music PR Hot List* (www.thebuzzfactor.com).

What we deal with in this chapter, though, is *how* you go about contacting the media.

Key Question: What good is having a hot list of radio station program directors and music magazine editors if the approach you take to reach them does more harm than good? That's the problem we're going to overcome in the following pages. So let's start off with one of the biggest mistakes you're probably making right now:

You're not sending effective messages to the media – messages that inspire media people to act on what you send them

Having been involved in music for a couple of decades now, I can tell you without hesitation that most music marketing communications – fliers, bios, cover letters, web sites, e-mail messages, ads and more – are weak and ineffective.

That is, they don't perform the only function that any marketing communication should ever do: Get the person receiving it to *act* by calling you, faxing you, writing to you, e-mailing you or coming to your event. At the very least, the message should pave the way for your follow-up e-mail, direct mail piece or phone call at a later date.

Bottom Line: Simply getting your stuff in the mail is not your ultimate goal. That's where most so-called music marketers go wrong; they throw useless information into the world and hope it sticks on something.

But that's not how you'll be dealing with the media from now on, because now you know that it's your job to send marketing messages that grab attention and motivate the people receiving them to act!

How to offer your music-related message to the media so you get the most results in the least amount of time

Make no mistake. The only goal you should have when you design and create a flier, gig calendar, artist bio, cover letter, fact sheet or advertisement – whether you're sending it to a media person, club owner, industry pro or fan – is to get the person receiving it to respond. And preferably to respond NOW! But first you have to know what it is you want them to do and then inspire them to do it (in a firm, yet polite and professional manner).

That's why, before you contact anyone in the media, you must ask yourself the following questions:

Who will receive my music news-related message?

The type of person getting your marketing materials will determine how you motivate him or her to act. Music fans are inspired by the emotion your music creates within them, the image you portray, and the people they'll hang out with at your gigs. Music industry pros (managers, A&R reps, entertainment lawyers), on the other hand, are persuaded to act if the potential to make money and earn a better name for themselves is present.

But media people are a different breed. So what motivates them? What would get a music editor, freelance writer or radio station program director to get excited enough about you to contact you right away?

Which leads to the next question ...

How should I persuade media people to take action?

In a nutshell, media people are motivated by these four things:

1) **Amusing and entertaining their specific audiences.** The first duty for a writer, webmaster or disc jockey is not to help out your band. It's to do his best job to retain and increase his audience.

2) **Being the first one in their region or niche to "break" a new, up-and-coming act.** When media types earn the reputation of being on the cutting edge, it makes them feel good. They love to be on top of trends and ahead of the cultural curve.

3) **Not missing the boat on something that is generating a buzz.** While some editors and program directors like being on the leading edge, they still want to play it safe by turning their readers/listeners (and their paying advertisers) on to something that has already proven itself popular.

4) **Exposing something that is witty or creative enough to grab their attention.** Many hundreds of acts over the years have inspired the media to action with either a funny band name, unusual album title or other promotional gimmick. Acts such as Dread Zeppelin, the Dead Milk Men and Mojo Nixon come to mind. Do you have a clever gimmick? If you do, just make sure the novelty aspect will create a reputation you can live with for years to come.

What do I want media people to do when they receive my info?

Run-of-the-mill music promoters toss literature about themselves to the media and leave it up to the media person to decide what to do next. But you won't do this. Remember, with few exceptions, the only reason you invest time and money to correspond with someone about your music is to motivate them to act!

Therefore, you will spell out in your e-mail messages and cover letters, in no uncertain terms, what you want recipients to do. Call, write, fax, come to your gig, listen to your tape, wait for your follow-up call ... whatever it is, ask them politely, yet very specifically, to do it.

Note: That doesn't mean media people will automatically do what you ask – more often than not, they won't. But at least you will have answered that nagging but all-important question: What happens next?

When do I want media people to take action?

A few years ago, I received a press kit from a band member who wanted me to write about his band. It was similar to hundreds of other packages I've received over the years. The accompanying pitch letter went on and on about what his band had done, how much the letter-writer thought of himself and that he wanted to appear on the cover of *Spotlight*, the music magazine I published.

(*Note:* You should never ask for a "cover story" on your band. That's a decision the editor makes based on what's best for the publication, regardless of who asked for it.)

However, nowhere in this guy's letter did it ask me to do anything or specify what he'd do next to further the process along. In essence, he was saying, "Here's a bunch of stuff about me and my needs. Now it's your job to figure out what it is I want you to do now to stroke my inflated ego even more. It doesn't matter if I hear from you today, next month or next year, and you may not hear from me ever again. The thing that's most important is that I've given you more material to fill your trash can with!"

Lesson: This craziness must stop! If it seems I'm being hard on this guy, it's only to prove a point: Spell out all the things you have to offer media people and then kindly give them specific marching orders (in a casual and friendly manner) on what they should do next – or expect from you next – and what they get from you when they do it.

That's what effective music marketing is all about.

Action-inducing copywriting essentials

"Copy," in this context, is not something you do at Kinko's. Copy is the wording that appears on all of your promotional materials. Here are some golden nuggets to make your copy sparkle:

Don't use me-centered thinking

I know I've already covered this, but it's so important I want to stress it again: Stop talking so much about yourself in "I-Me-My" terms. Most band bios, cover letters and e-mail messages are littered with "I think this ... We did that ... I am ... We want ... I, I, I ..." Perhaps you're not clear about why this is important to you. You may be asking, "How else am *I* supposed to tell media people about *my* music?"

The answer: By focusing on what's in it for the media person! (If you're not sure what that is, review the four points earlier in this chapter.) The problem with so much of the plentiful me-centered copy around is that it is practically void of the most important marketing word of all: "You."

Reality: Let's face it. Most people are motivated by some level of greed; they naturally focus on themselves. Experts say it's an ancient human survival instinct left over from the caveman era. And that's fine. It's not a crime to put a priority on your goals and aspirations. But when you communicate with others, it's important to resist the urge to focus on yourself. To get what you want, you must cater to other people's goals and aspirations. You have to figure out how your needs can be met by helping others meet their own needs.

From now on, I'd like you to keep in mind that what motivates media people (and all people, for that matter) is what they get out of various relationships. Whenever you communicate with someone – whether on the Internet, in person, on the phone or in writing – he or she is either consciously or unconsciously asking, "So what's in this for me, bub?"

Of course, you can react to this reality of human nature by thinking how unfair it is. Or you can use this knowledge to your advantage to get what you really want out of your music career.

Bad Example: When communicating with a member of the media, don't write something like, "I have a good band. We have gotten airplay in our region. I would love for you to give us some exposure in your state, too. We could really use it." The most common response to this type of marketing is: "So what? Who cares what you could use? Why should I add to my already busy schedule to help you?"

But what if you tried this approach with your copy?

"You could be the first one in your market to expose the XYZ Band! With college airplay on 15 stations in 7 states, now is a great time to spread the word to your audience. Your listeners/readers will thank you for sharing us with them – and you'll be glad you did. Call 555-1234 right now to get your own copy of XYZ's new CD and a FREE T-shirt. Call 24 hours a day, 7 days a week. Debbie, the XYZ answering machine, is standing by."

Even though the preceding copy is a little over the top with tongue-in-cheek humor, hopefully you can see how "you"-oriented it is and how much more effective it could be than the example before it.

It's the same band and the same information, just a better way to present it to get results. The former piece of ... er, copy ... is ego-driven and bland. The latter speaks directly to the media person and what's in it for her – it addresses her needs, not yours. Plus it offers her a playful call to action to get the goodies the band has waiting for her ... if she only calls now!

Are you starting to get the picture? I've taken up a good amount of space to address this issue, but I think it's an important one. Hopefully, you do too.

Before we wrap this up, here are a few more action-inducing ideas to use in your messages to the music media:

Include your name, address and phone number

This should be obvious, but you'd be surprised how many music marketers overlook it. Along with inspiring a media person to action, you must include the methods by which to contact you. Do you want a media person to call you? Send an e-mail or return post card? Make sure your name, address, phone number, e-mail and web site are clearly noted within your message. Again, you want to motivate these people to action, and then make it easy for them to connect with you.

Consider using a response coupon

You've no doubt seen these used in ads and fliers for a variety of products and services. Typically, a response coupon is outlined by a broken border, implying that the reader should cut it out and use it. Inside the border are lines to write in a name, address and phone number. The most effective response coupons start with a place to put a check mark and a sentence or two at the top that reads ...

"[ ] Yes! I'm ready to take action to get the benefit you're offering. Please send me free details right away."

Why not use this technique yourself? Marketing research indicates that simply having a response coupon on a marketing document increases the rate of response – even if the person responding doesn't actually fill it out and mail it. In other words, response coupons act as a visual stimulus that psychologically triggers the reader to act. Therefore, include your phone number and e-mail address near the response coupon section of your mailing piece. That way, the coupon alone will help inspire the person to contact you, but other contact options are there in case he or she wants your new release or media kit sooner.

Include testimonials, sales charts, play lists, review comments, article reprints, etc.

As I've already mentioned, you telling a media person how wonderful you are will get you nowhere fast. But there is a way to impress media people without having to use God-awful, ill-fated, me-centered copy. The key is to get respected, third-party sources to say something good about you, and then use those positive quotes to reinforce the fact that you are worth writing about or being given radio airplay.

Best Approach: Starting right now, you should pursue all opportunities for free press and airplay, beginning with your local papers and radio stations. Whenever a review or article is written about your musical act, clip and copy the piece and add it to your press package. Also, when your indie release ends up on a station play list or regional sales chart, get a copy of it and do the same thing.

Important: Effective music marketing includes an ongoing process of pursuing and compiling third-party endorsements of your worthiness – and then using those comments to get what you want from the media.

You should also approach local disc jockeys, program directors, editors, writers – even agents, nightclub owners and recording studio owners – and ask them for a comment you can use in your media kit. Before long, you'll have a whole collection of testimonials (from people other than your friends, family and yourself) on the success you've produced thus far, not to mention your potential for larger-scale success.

Offer something free if media people respond now

Along with encouraging media people to contact you to get your CD or press kit, why not offer something else free to the first 25 callers. (Why not? It works for radio stations, why not your music marketing efforts?) Give away a T-shirt, poster, coffee mug, condom ... whatever you can think of to help inspire a quick response!

There you have it – a quick course on how to make any communication you have with the media a more productive one.

Key Question: Now what happens? Will you remain part of the majority of music marketers – people who say they really want to promote their music on a wider scale ... but never get past talking about it?

Or will you be part of the top five percent of the music community – people who have a true passion for the art and craft of making music? People who also know that being successful means taking that burning desire and belief in yourself and combining it with a healthy, regular dose of action.

Are you that type of person?

Only you can answer that. But whether you're in a band, run a record label or publicity department, or have a music-related product or service to promote, I encourage you to start putting these media exposure techniques to work right away. The worst thing that could happen is that you'd move one step closer to achieving your musical goals.

And that's not a bad place to be.

Chapter 5

The First Question You Must Answer When Promoting Your Music

I'm going to use this entire chapter to deal with one subject because I think it's vital to the success of your music promotion efforts. Every day I see the same mistake being made in this area and feel I owe it to you to drive this crucial point home.

Suppose you walked into your local record store and one of the employees (a complete stranger to you) came up and handed you a box filled with CDs and said, "Here, these are extra promo copies. You can have any CD you want out of the box."

Now let's pretend that you were not familiar with any of these artists. As you picked up each CD to consider whether or not you wanted it, what would be the first question to pop into your head? In other words, what basic question would you need to answer first before you could make an intelligent (and quick) decision on which one you'd take?

Would it be "Who produced this CD?"

No.

Would it be "What record label put this out?"

No.

How about "Where is this act from?"

No.

Would it be "What do these musicians think of their own music?"

No.

Hopefully, you've come to the same conclusion that I have. The first question that anyone asks when encountering new music is:

"What kind of music is this?"

I've used this box of free CDs example to make a point: This is exactly the same position that music editors, radio program directors, A&R people and music publishers are in when they receive your unsolicited recordings along with dozens of others. Even though it's great to think that everyone already knows who you are and what you do, the sad truth is that most of your contacts will be clueless. That's why giving them the first and most important clue up front is essential.

Human beings need some way to process information and file it away in the proper place in their heads before proceeding to any follow-up questions, such as "Where is this band from?" or "What unique spin do they put on this genre?" Without creating a mental category or comparison to something fans are already familiar with, it's nearly impossible to get to these important follow-up questions. And if you can't move this sorting-out process along in a swift manner, your music marketing efforts end up dead in the water.

Why, then, do so many people who promote music either ignore answering this fundamental question – "What kind of music is this?" – or bury the answer so deep in their promotion materials that the reader gives up out of frustration before ever uncovering it?

Unless you are (or are working with) a well-known artist, the people receiving your promo kits will be in the dark as to who you are and what you play. Your job, therefore, is to answer that first all-important question right off the bat: "What kind of music is this?" It should be one of the first things people see when viewing your press package.

Here's an example I randomly pulled out of an overflowing box of review CDs years ago when I was a music editor. After opening the package, the first thing I see is a cover letter. Here's how it reads (I've changed the name of the person, label and band to protect the misguided):

"My name is John Jones, vice president of Widget Records, here in New York. I'm writing to announce that one of our bands, the Losers, will be playing in St. Louis on July 24."

It's important to Jones that he announces who he is and what he does right off the bat. I'm sure this makes him feel good about himself. But how does this introduction move him closer to his goal of getting media coverage for the poor Losers? At least I know about the St. Louis date, something that should matter to me. But since I don't know what kind of music this is, I'm not impressed. On to the next paragraph.

"The Losers' music is already on national college and commercial radio."

Excellent. His mother must be very proud of him. But is this jazz radio? Alternative radio? Polka radio? Ten stations? Eight hundred stations? Huh? I'm still being kept in the dark.

"The Losers are a new band founded in 1997 in New York City. These shows are part of the year-long tour to promote their debut album."

More senseless background details before I even know what kind of music this band plays. But one thing I do know is that Jones sure likes talking about his band and its accomplishments. Now I'm starting to doze off. But I keep reading anyway.

"The Losers' music combines Celtic violin with punk-influenced distorted guitars and melodic rock vocals ..."

What? A description of the music? Say it isn't so! And I only had to wait till the fourth paragraph to get it. And it ends up being a pretty cool description: Celtic violin with punk guitars. Now that's different. That's something I'd like to pop in the CD player and check out. What a great media hook for the band.

Unfortunately, the label's vice president has done the group a disservice by burying this vital piece of information in a dreary cover letter. Most media people would have given up on it long before they got to the intriguing description.

But this never occurred to Jones. It was much more important for him to pound his chest and proclaim his name, title, city and the fact that his as-yet-undefined band was getting radio airplay. What a missed opportunity! Don't make this same error.

How much better it would have been if his letter went something like this:

"Dear Bob,

When we first told people we had signed a band that combined Celtic violins with distorted punk guitars and melodic rock vocals, they told us we were crazy. But we proved them all wrong with the Losers, a band that is now on a major roll. Last month alone, over 325 college stations around the country were playing cuts off the band's new self-titled CD. And now you can experience the Losers yourself when they come to St. Louis on July 24. I think your readers would get a kick out of hearing about this unusual Celtic/violin/punk/melodic mixture ..."

This version pulls you in and lets you know what you're dealing with quickly and interestingly – as opposed to Jones's dry meanderings.

Now take a look at some of the promotional tools you're using now. What's the first thing you see? Your address? The band members' names? The record label name? Some vague reference to how impressive your music is without a specific definition of it?

Stop beating around the bush and start getting to the heart of the matter. Media and industry people are partly overworked and partly lazy. Don't shroud your message in mystery, hoping it will tease people and make them read further. Remember this important rule: No one will ever be as interested in reading your press materials as you are. So give them what they need up front, fast and simple.

And answer the most important question first: "What kind of music is this?"

Chapter 6

How One Solo Artist Used the Internet to Sell 4,000 CDs

We can all learn a lot from John Taglieri, a singer/songwriter from New Jersey who in two short years transformed himself from being a frustrated veteran musician to being a one-man success story in the wired world.

"I spent a lot of time early in my career chasing down a dream that I thought was always just beyond my reach," says Taglieri of his years in the bar band trenches. "I had burned out on the original scene and needed a break." After a couple of years, though, the itch to create music returned. "Only this time, I wanted it my way."

Taglieri went the do-it-yourself route and wrote and recorded a solo CD, called *Leap of Faith*. "The CD, aptly titled, was my leap of faith to see if I could really make it in the business," he says.

Since the release of his CD, Taglieri has sold about 4,000 units, toured, performed at music conferences, landed two major sponsors and has been signed to an indie label. He also has investors paying for his next album and upcoming tour. How did he come so far so quickly?

Searching for the right avenue

"When I released the CD, I took out ads in the local papers, got the CD in all the major local stores on consignment and tried my hardest to promote it," he explains. "I did all the traditional methods of promotion."

Taglieri then landed an appearance on one of the biggest morning radio shows in New York. Sales went through the roof that week, with almost all of the stores selling out of their stock. But as his appearance on the show faded into memory, so did the sales.

"The problem was, I couldn't figure out how to keep it going," he says. "As a solo artist, I had no band to go and book clubs with, so touring was not an option at that point."

The ambitious musician did something during this period that proved to be a turning point: He acquired a computer and started learning what the Internet was all about. Once he realized the potential that sat at his fingertips, there was no stopping him.

"The Internet has created a whole new world out there for singer/songwriters, bands and musicians in general. What I learned over the next 18 months, and still am learning, is just how valuable the Internet can be."

Taglieri's approach to cyber promotion is fairly simple. He explains: "I'm a pop-rock songwriter. My music has been compared to Journey and Bon Jovi. It has a 1980s style with a newer rock feel. So I started searching the Web for any sites that catered to my type of music. I got listed on some of the generic music web sites, but I felt the genre-specific sites offered a better chance of getting exposure and good reviews."

Important lesson: Focus on sites that cater to your style of music. You'll never be all things to all people, so spend your limited time concentrating on sites where you have the best chance of connecting with the audience.

"I would find one web site for my type of music and contact them about the possibilities of reviews and promotion, then go to their links page and go to every site on that page. I kept up this routine for every site I went to," he says. "For every one I visited, I wound up on 25 more, which led me to 75 more. Before long, I had made contact with dozens of webmasters who were willing to mention me or do a review."

Time-released success

Progress was slow at first, but things began to pick up steam. "Within a few months, the ball was rolling. The first few reviews came out and were very positive. This opened the door to other sites that were reluctant to let me in. Once they saw me getting good reviews, they were willing to give it a try."

Taglieri spent from six to eight hours a day on the Internet while working a full-time job. When he wasn't at work, he was on the Net promoting his music. Over a 12-month period, he racked up more than 50 reviews. He attributes his success to putting in the time, being pleasantly persistent, and having patience and determination.

I've long advocated Taglieri's personal, one-on-one approach. Even against the backdrop of today's quick-fix era, this time-honored philosophy still pays dividends.

I encourage you to start a simple database of web sites (and the specific human contacts at each one) that are dedicated to your style of music.

How to start your online search

Here are a list of music directories where you can begin your search. Of course, as Taglieri will tell, it takes time and commitment to make it work.

Google - Music Directories
http://directory.google.com/Top/Arts/Music/Directories/

Yahoo! - Music Web Directories
http://dir.yahoo.com/Entertainment/Music/Web_Directories/

MusicDish Genome Project
www.musicdish.com/genome

Music Business Solutions: Resource Directory
www.mbsolutions.com/resource

Rock Source Music Directory
www.rocksource.net

More music marketing wisdom from Taglieri

"Everything in life basically works on the same principal: customer service. You have to treat everyone you come in contact with as a customer," he says. "You want to be treated well for the things you do, and so do the webmasters of the sites we all beg and expect reviews from. Give them every courtesy you can."

Taglieri also sends every webmaster a thank-you e-mail telling them how much he appreciates any reviews he gets, good or bad. "This may seem silly, but I can't stress how important it is. Many webmasters e-mail me back saying how much they appreciated it. Their common complaint is that artists take them for granted, and once they get the review, they never hear from them again, except when they need something else."

Lesson: Music promotion on or off the Internet is a two-way street. If all you ever do is ask for something from your music biz connections, eventually they may stop giving. Ask yourself what you can do for the people who help you. Perhaps it's giving their 'zine a plug in your newsletter or adding their site to your links page. Maybe you can even pass along a note about a helpful web site or news story you've run across.

"I make it a point every month or so to send a hello e-mail to everyone who's ever reviewed me," Taglieri adds. "This serves two purposes. First, it lets them know I'm thinking about them and stopping by their sites, which I do. I can never forget who's done things for me because I see their names every time I look at my press kit. Second, it keeps you in their minds, which can lead to more promotion."

Staying connected to people who can help you

Even if you're sold on the idea of keeping in touch, it's easy to get sidetracked. If you're a forgetful type, use a free service to send you an e-mail reminder message at certain intervals. Three services to consider are:

Memo to Me
www.memotome.com

Remember It
www.rememberit.com

EMinders
www.eminders.com

Also, to keep track of the growing number of contacts in your music database, you'll need to store this information somewhere. You should use some type of contact management software, which allows you to enter details into separate fields such as web site name, URL, contact name, contact's e-mail, description of the site, etc. Here are a few applications to consider:

ACT
www.act.com

FileMaker
www.filemaker.com

MyMailList
www.avanquestusa.com/products/mymld

After several months of steady web exposure, Taglieri started getting more requests for online interviews and feature stories. He also began winning web site awards and being listed on some sites' "best" lists.

"Recognition like that enhances your exposure because now you are front page news on music web sites, instead of just a listing in their databases," Taglieri says. "What it also did was create a buzz for sales. My web site started getting a lot more hits and sales picked up dramatically."

Taglieri eventually embarked on a self-booked, 23-city tour. He got press in 14 of the 23 cities and sold more than 400 CDs by the time the tour came to an end.

"With my name on many web sites and magazines, I was beginning to get approached by small indie labels both in the U.S. and Europe. That's the beauty of the Internet. The world is as close as right next door. There are very few barriers."

More recently, Taglieri inked a deal with an indie label and landed a sponsorship with Ovation Guitars.

What is success worth to you?

"It all comes down to one thing: How bad do you want it and how much are you willing to sacrifice for it? I gave up going out and partying, having a big social life and many other things because it was far more important for me to be working on making a name for myself and getting my career off the ground. You can't be afraid of promotion and you can't be afraid of trying. The only thing I lost was a few hangovers, and in my book, that's not such a bad thing."

Taglieri believes that anyone who goes after his or her dreams and let's nothing get in the way can be proud, even if he or she doesn't ultimately reach the highest pinnacle of success. At least you gave it your all.

"Awards, accolades, great press, interviews, sponsorships, record deals – it's all out there for the taking," he adds. "You just have to learn how to go after things. Nothing is handed to you, and when it is, it generally won't last. But if you work for it and do it right, success will last. And it will mean so much more because you'll know you put your heart and soul into it."

To find out more about John Taglieri and his music, visit his web site at www.johntaglieri.com.

Chapter 7

Avoid the Most Common Artist Web Site Design Mistakes

C.J. Chilvers may not be a web site designer *per se*, but during the course of running www.musicjournalist.com he's seen plenty of music-related web sites – online 'zines, music news sources, artist sites and more. This in-depth exposure to music-themed Internet real estate has given him some strong opinions on music web site design – the good, the bad and the ugly.

"I've spent countless hours staring at poorly designed sites searching for their vitals – What is this site about? Who do I contact? Etcetera. Over the past two years I've gotten to know these design mistakes quite well," Chilvers says.

"Many people say that design is an art and is therefore subjective," he continues. "However, web design includes information architecture, copywriting, customer service and a host of other elements that can be objectively studied. Mistakes in web design are, for the most part, obstacles placed between the visitor and the content they're seeking. With music-related sites, that content can be anything from articles and photos to calendars and streaming media."

Throughout the following questions and answers, Chilvers describes the most common mistakes he encounters – mistakes that he says frustrate users and mar otherwise interesting music web sites.

What's the number one problem with music web site design?

Lack of clarity and purpose. It seems as though many music sites exist for no particular reason; they just exist. The authors assume that we already know why they exist and why it's important to visit regularly. There may be news about obscure bands, but no mention of what kind of music the site covers. There may be information about the "local scene" without a mention of what city that scene is located in. Assume nothing of your visitors. Make your reason for being online clear.

What are your thoughts on Macromedia Flash intros?

Few subjects cause the kind of heated arguments that Flash consistently does. Supporters insist that they refuse to cater to the lowest common denominator; that Flash is just another form of expression. Fine. Do it on your own time or in the name of art. Who is your target audience? Most likely it's not other web designers, so getting their approval isn't important. Getting the approval of your visitors and fans is important.

Popular band sites, for example, have visitors that return several times a week. To have to wade through Flash intros and splash pages every visit is frustrating and annoying, especially when you consider that many visitors have slower, dial-up connections. Flash can be used for good but rarely is. You should never add a design element to your site just to show that you can.

Any other pet peeves?

Yes. Multi-colored backgrounds. The two most important factors to consider when presenting your written content are readability and printability. Both are killed easily by bad backgrounds. Readability is enhanced by contrast. It's much easier to read black text on a white background than pink text on a green background. Also, using a patterned background is always guaranteed to confuse a reader.

By far the most common background mistake in music sites, though, is the use of a black background. Such a mistake is partially redeemable by using white text for high contrast. However, if you believe your content is valuable enough for visitors to print, you should stick to black or dark-colored text on a white background.

What about feedback forms and contact information?

The best way to make your site totally impersonal is to use feedback forms. Though mostly used on big sites, like SPIN and Q, smaller sites are also frequent abusers of the form. What's wrong with forms? They make things easier for the webmaster, and that's part of the problem. You should be worried about making things easier for the visitor, not yourself. Instead of using forms, just supply your e-mail address.

In addition to providing a contact name, title and e-mail address, be sure to make your contact information perfectly clear. This may be the most common problem I've encountered on music sites – no clue on who to contact.

How will you know what your visitors want if you don't provide contact information? How will you know about problems with your site, like typos, errors and technical problems? What if your site isn't viewable on your visitors' browsers?

Contact information should be up front and complete. What you are saying by not providing this information is, "I don't want to be troubled by my visitors." Unless you're ashamed of your content, you should never hesitate to offer your contact info.

I hear you're also not a big fan of banner ads.

Banner ads, unless they are very targeted and useful to readers, are usually ignored. The small amount of revenue they provide is almost never worth the costs, which include decreased speed of navigation and ugliness. According to e-commerce experts, the single most important technical feature of a web site is its speed.

How important is it to update a music site?

That's the first thing I look for at a site. You'd be surprised how many online 'zines haven't been touched in over a year. You may think you're reading an interview with the Deftones about their latest album, but you're actually reading an interview about an album they released years ago.

Ever wonder why there are so many thousands of listings for e-zines at large music sites but only hundreds in the www.musicjournalist.com publications directory? Because we look for dates! Check the copyright date at music news sites. If the site's copyright says 1999, it's probably a dead e-zine that's never been deleted by the owner.

You want to hear something really sad? Some music sites offer news without dates. Here's a tip: It's only "news" if it's new. Make sure your visitors know how new your news is. It'll give them a reason to keep coming back.

What do you think of band sites that automatically play a song as soon as you enter the site?

Don't force sound on your visitors. Far too many music sites force visitors to download a sound file when they first visit the site, usually in conjunction with a Flash intro. Why not just come right out and say, "We do not value your time. You will sit there and wait until we are good and ready to show you our site." Let visitors decide if they want to take the time to download and play sound files.

Any final tips on designing a user-friendly music site?

This last one is more about attitude. It's very common for a site to announce arrogantly, "Best if viewed with IE 4.0+ at 1024 x 768." Your site is best viewed in whatever way your visitors feel like viewing it. Making demands on the way your visitors view your site is like McDonald's making demands on the way its customers eat Big Macs. Be happy that they're showing up! Give them a reason to keep showing up.

Web design is a multi-faceted topic. We've only scratched the surface with this short chapter. Here are several online resources to help you register, host, design and operate a successful web site:

To register a domain name ...

Go Daddy
www.godaddy.com

DirectNic
www.directnic.com

For web site hosting ...

Host Baby
www.hostbaby.com

Web Hosting Directory
www.webhostdir.com

eHostingBiz
www.ehostingbiz.com

For web design tips and tools ...

Website Tips
www.websitetips.com

Grantastic Designs
www.grantasticdesigns.com

How to Build Websites
www.how-to-build-websites.com

Killer Sites
www.killersites.com

To find a web designer ...

Music Web Designer Database
www.hostbaby.com/wddb/search

Guerrilla Music Marketing Activity Worksheets – #1

What are your top 5 skills (musical and otherwise)?

1. _____

2. _____

3. _____

4. _____

5. _____

What aspects of your musical career really drive you?

_____

_____

_____

_____

List some of your past or current successes:

_____

_____

_____

_____

_____

List some of your failures and, most importantly, what you learned from each one:

_____

_____

_____

_____

_____

What are your top 5 long-term goals:

1. _____
2. _____
3. _____
4. _____
5. _____

What are your top 5 short-term goals:

1. _____
2. _____
3. _____
4. _____
5. _____

What obstacles might you face along the way to reaching your goals?

_____
_____
_____
_____

How will you effectively deal with those obstacles when they arise?

_____
_____
_____
_____

List the people, organizations and information sources that may help you achieve your goals:

_____
_____
_____
_____
_____
_____

Describe – in detail – your ideal fan:

_____

_____

_____

_____

_____

What truly motivates your fans to support you (what's the benefit to them)?

_____

_____

_____

_____

_____

Write a Brand Identity Statement (BIS) of 10 words or less to describe your music and image:

_____

_____

_____

_____

_____

What industry people might you approach for a positive comment you can use in your press materials?

_____

_____

_____

_____

_____

_____

Make a list of web sites ideally suited to your music:

_____

_____

_____

_____

What online music promotion tactics would work best for you?

_____

_____

_____

_____

What web site design elements would be ideal to promote your unique style of music?

_____

_____

_____

_____

List 10 things you can do in the next week to start moving toward your music goals:

1. _____
2. _____
3. _____
4. _____
5. _____
6. _____
7. _____
8. _____
9. _____
10. _____

Chapter 8

35 Ways to Sell a Lot More of Your CDs, Tapes, DVDs and Music Merchandise

You've put a lot of time and effort into writing good original songs, committing them to finished tracks in the studio, crafting the artwork and packaging, and arranging for your CD, tape or DVD to finally be manufactured.

Many musicians describe the feeling of seeing their slickly packaged final creation for the first time: It's a wonderful sensation of accomplishment. They feel like shouting at the top of their lungs to let the world know about this great thing they've got to offer.

That's why it's difficult to figure out why so many music makers drop the ball at this point. Sure, they want to get recognition from hordes of people who have been touched by their music. And, let's face it, they wouldn't mind making some good money selling their product, too. So why do artists continue to manufacture 1,000 units only to have 900 of them sit in a closet and gather dust?

The answer is simple: These artists haven't learned effective methods for marketing their releases. Also, they haven't done their homework and haven't discovered the many resources available to help them sell their CDs. Are you one of these people? If so, don't worry. There's help within the pages ahead.

What follows are 35 solid ideas and resources to expand your thinking and help you sell more of your independent releases.

1) Get committed

Not to an insane asylum, but to becoming an independent music marketer – instead of just a music producer. Unless you're simply making music for your immediate friends and family (which is worthy in itself), you're going to have to extend your skills to include more than songwriting and recording techniques.

Far too many musically creative people feel that if they just come up with great music, the world will beat a path to their door. While this approach might seem to work for a select few, most songwriters and musicians have to work a little harder to get their music not only noticed but bought in bulk by enthusiastic music fans.

Important: The first step in your efforts to sell more of your CDs, DVDs and music merchandise is to decide right now that you will spend as much time and energy marketing your musical pride and joy as you do creating it. This means you are eager to indulge in the art of researching your market, networking with people who can help you accomplish your sales goals and, ultimately, becoming as inspired by exposing your music as you are by playing it.

2) Know who your fans are and why they buy from you

Yes, this is covered in another chapter, but let's emphasize it again: How would you describe the ideal consumer of your music? And what inspires him or her to buy your CDs and merchandise? If you can't answer these questions, you may have a tough battle (not to mention a closet full of CDs) ahead of you.

Acts that develop loyal followings usually have a specific musical focus and image that their fans identify with so strongly, they pack the group's shows and buy tons of their releases. The magnet that draws these fans is the personality of the band, combined with a sound, look and image that supports it.

Get a handle on what attitude, sound and image you portray – and how those things positively affect the way your fans feel. Knowing this will help you position your act for maximum exposure ... and sales! **Important note:** Make sure the image you promote is a true part of who you are. Copping an identity only because you think it will sell will cause your career to fall apart quicker than you can say, "Milli Vanilli."

3) Create new music categories and distribution channels

You can add real marketing muscle to your releases if you can develop a fresh approach to defining them. New Age music, for instance, is often marketed through spiritual "rock shops" as a sonic stimulus people can use to relax, meditate and unwind. Some labels have thematic releases that are packaged with books on the same subject, which opens up bookstore sales – a whole new method of distribution.

Another example: The Memphis, TN-based Hands On Inc. promotes Driving Music. It's a self-created category of music specially recorded and mastered for car stereo systems. The clever people behind this concept say the process, which they call "Precision Mastering," makes the best use of the peculiar acoustic environment of the automobile – without needing extra equipment.

Added Advantage: By creating this new category, Hands On Inc. also opened up a new retail distribution source: They market the releases through auto centers.

Can you think of a fresh distribution channel that would work for you?

4) Package your releases as a related series

Jazz musician Cole Broderick came up with the idea to write a cycle of four CDs based on the changing seasons of Saratogo Springs, NY, where he spends a good deal of his time. The first release in the series, the aptly titled *Springtime in Saratoga*, was followed up with releases relating to summer, autumn and winter. What a great concept.

Packaging a series of related titles brings with it a lot of advantages, including:

- **It encourages repeat buying.** Music fans who purchase one in the series will be more inclined to get the entire set – if they like what they hear on the first one, of course.

- **Distributors and retailers love it.** They know they'll have more than one product coming from you. Plus they realize each release encourages more sales of the others.

- **It makes for a great media hook.** This unique approach to your music makes you stand out when editors and writers are making story decisions.

Consider the series method when planning your future recording projects.

5) Make the most of live shows

Hands down, live shows are one of your best ways to promote and sell a new release. However, many musicians think it's uncool to repeatedly plug their "product" at gigs.

Reality: You want people to come to your shows because they like your music, right? If they've taken the time to set aside an evening to experience your live show, wouldn't many of them also want to take your recorded music home? Of course. Don't deny them that experience. And don't deny yourself the monetary rewards of selling more of your music.

Live shows create the perfect buying environment. People in the audience experience your music and personality firsthand. You touch them in the most direct way. At the same time, a busy club or concert hall can have a lot of distractions.

That's why you need to be more aggressive and hawk your wares regularly from the stage, as long as you do it in a cool and confident way.

6) Print and distribute a band newsletter

Most bands pass out fliers or calendars at their live shows, but fliers get tossed in the trash pretty quickly and usually don't help a band's efforts in selling more CDs and merchandise. The solution is to publish a newsletter that's filled with tidbits of information on your band and the releases you have for sale. (I also advocate publishing an e-mail newsletter; but this section specifically refers to a paper newsletter you hand out at shows.)

The most effective band newsletters use plenty of humor and display the members' personalities. By having fun items of interest in your newsletter, people will hang onto it longer and share it with friends. Plus, you can include a convenient order form and announce where fans can get your cool stuff online and in stores.

Added Benefit: You can also use your newsletter to sell T-shirts, sweatshirts, posters, caps, stickers and all sorts of revenue-producing band merchandise.

7) When you do print, radio and TV interviews, give something away

As you know, a great way to build up a following is to compile and use a mailing list. (You do have one, don't you?) Make no mistake, your mailing list can be a powerful tool in stimulating sales. But live gigs and your web site are not the only places to collect those lucrative names and addresses.

When you do media interviews, you're reaching perhaps thousands of potential fans (and buyers). Make the best use of that opportunity by giving something away to readers, listeners or viewers – your newsletter, catalog, sticker, band comic book, novelty condom ... anything to inspire music fans to connect with you. You can have people go to your web site, call a band hotline number or call the station while you're in the studio.

Bottom line: Give fans a reason to connect with you and hand over their contact info in exchange for your cool freebie.

8) Give something away when you run paid ads

Likewise, when you are paying for advertising (whether in print, on the radio or online), don't waste the chance to connect with more fans. Offer that same free item mentioned above in all of your ads!

Lesson: This strategy gives you more control over the marketing process. Most artists and record labels simply throw their name out into the public. Then they hope and pray someone will take notice and be intrigued enough to drop everything else they're doing, hop in the car, drive to the retail outlet and purchase their record. I ask you: What percentage of people interested in your ad are really going to do that?

Therefore, you – being the creative music promoter that you are – won't take that roll-of-the-dice approach. From now on, you'll take control and gather the names and addresses (both street and e-mail) of people who are interested in your style of music. And you'll gather those details by offering potential fans something free in exchange for revealing their personal contact information.

Once you have these vital fan names and addresses, you have the power to gently prod and directly inspire them – through your regular follow-up communications – to take the next logical step: buying your CD, tape, DVD or other piece of merchandise.

Don't be a victim of chance when it comes to your music promotion. Grab the reigns and take control of the process!

9) Offer radio stations free copies to use as on-air giveaways

Media folks love to give away stuff to their audiences. So don't be shy about asking your local college and community stations if they'd give away your new CD on the air. Of course, you should also offer to come in, do an interview and play tracks off the CD (or perform live) to tie in with the giveaway. Be sure to let listeners know where they can go (online and off) to purchase your CD. Radio exposure of any kind can be good for your notoriety and the sales of your recorded music.

10) Give copies to record stores for in-store play

This may seem obvious, but a lot of "record producers" overlook this important marketing technique. A record store is the perfect place to capture the attention of music fans. Customers visit these establishments to do only one thing: listen to and buy music!

Ask any record store clerk how many times customers come up and ask, "Who is this playing over the speakers right now?" Get smart and start meeting with store managers and giving away free promotional copies to stores where your release is available.

11) Arrange for record store appearances, autograph sessions and unplugged performances

I know what you're thinking: "Record store appearance? That would be awfully pompous of me!" Not so fast. The national touring acts aren't the only musicians worthy of such gimmicks. Setting up an in-store appearance gives you weeks of exposure in the store in the form of fliers promoting the date. In-store events also get people talking and, in the case of unplugged performances, get your music to the ears of record-buying consumers who might never have heard you otherwise. Remember, consumers have to hear you before they'll buy.

12) Offer local record stores a free package-stuffer

Many retail businesses stuff a flier or discount coupon into customers' bags along with their purchases. Wouldn't it be great to get a record store to put your small flier into all its customers' packages? Your message would go directly to the music-buying public!

Print some professionally designed inserts promoting your CD. Visit record stores and ask managers to use the inserts. You might find sympathetic owners who will do it simply to help you out. But you'll quite likely meet resistance with this unusual request. What then? Call it quits? Hardly.

Hot Tip: Make the package insert two-sided. Offer to put the store's message on one side and your message on the other. You pay for printing the whole thing. That way, the store gets free promotion and an incentive to stuff them – and you get lots of direct exposure for very little cost.

13) Find alternate ways to market your band

Is there a non-music publication or offbeat type of retail store that admirers of your style of music might patronize? If so, you might consider reaching potential new fans through these unlikely means.

Example: BMG moved a lot of hard rock and metal sampler cassettes by advertising them through, of all things, comic books. The tapes featured cuts from such bands as 21 Guns, Babylon AD and the Rollins Band. Readers could order the samplers via a toll-free 800 number.

"There is a significant portion of the comic-reading and record-buying public that overlaps," said a senior VP of marketing at BMG. A number of the comic book respondents bought full albums based on hearing tracks on the sampler – and that's exactly what BMG wanted.

How can you do something similar with your music on a smaller scale?

14) Create incentives to buy

There are a number of effective ways to upgrade your fans and inspire additional sales. The trick is to dangle more alluring benefits in front of them while their interest level is running high. This isn't being manipulative, by the way. You're simply giving people an opportunity to get more of the great musical stuff you have to offer.

Example: Let's say someone buys your band's latest CD by mail. The average music marketer would stick the CD in a package and send it off. Period. Maybe later, he or she might send a flier of other merchandise. But why wait?

Better: The smart Guerrilla Music Marketer sends the CD along with a flier listing all other available products (past releases, T-shirts, caps, posters, even CDs by other comparable bands). In addition, the package would include a certificate stating something along the lines of:

"Thanks for your order. To show our appreciation, please use this 10 percent-off coupon on your next purchase of band merchandise. As an added bonus, order within the next 30 days and take an entire 20 percent off. It's our way of saying thanks for supporting our music."

15) Create a mini-catalog or web site featuring several similar groups

Contact other similarly styled bands in your region that have CDs available. Pool your resources and print a low-cost catalog featuring all the bands' CDs (or create a flier that directs people to a web site that serves the same purpose). Hand out the catalogs at your gigs and promote them to the media. A catalog or web site of several bands sharing the same theme carries a lot more weight with both fans and the media than a flier selling your products alone. Use this hook to build your mailing list and sell more of your own releases – while helping other bands in your region.

16) Produce sampler CDs as a promotional tool

People need to hear your music before they can decide if they like it enough to buy your CD. Getting enough radio airplay to sufficiently expose your music can be a challenge. Sampler CDs are one solution. Take two or three songs from your full-length CD and put them on a sampler CD. Ask record stores to give them away. Use them as a freebie for people who sign up on your mailing list at gigs. Send a press release to the media announcing that the CDs are available to anyone by mail for two or three dollars to cover shipping.

17) Make a John Hancock offer

When you first make a new release available, consider offering a limited number of autographed copies. **Best Advice:** Make the number of signed copies small and limited (perhaps 50 to 100). This will inspire serious fans to order even faster. Of course, you can actually deliver more than you promise and autograph more than the number you say is available. But by making it a limited offer, fans will be more motivated to send their money your way. (By the way, John Hancock was the signer with the largest signature on the *Declaration of Independence*.)

18) Use a point-of-purchase display

Looking for a professional way to display your CDs and cassettes in record stores? Make use of cardboard countertop displays. Ask record store employees if they have displays they don't need anymore. Fix them up and decorate them with your artwork. If you want to purchase brand-new displays, check out the following companies:

DISCmarket
www.discmarket.com

CD Stands
www.cdstands.com

Video and CD Counter Displays
www.counterdisplay.com/16CD.htm

Cactus Containers
www.cactuscontainers.com

19) Get on Bestseller, Most Popular and Most Downloaded Lists

True music fans hate to miss out on the latest craze within their preferred genre. One way fans discover what new music is worth buying is by looking over the growing number of popularity lists on various music web sites. These lists come in all shapes and sizes: Top Sellers, Most Listened To, Most Popular Downloads, etc. The higher your ranking on these lists, the more attention you draw to yourself.

So how can you get visibility on these lists and boost your sales? Well, writing and recording a fantastic song and getting it out there is the first step. An audience will find a killer song through word of mouth, etc. But you can help things along by asking your fans and friends to visit, vote, download, listen or whatever it takes to help you rank higher on these lists.

Suggestion: Pick one such list on one site in a category where you can make an impact. Ask the people on your mailing list to visit that site and take the required action on the same day or during the same week. This concentrated effort may be all it takes to get you to move higher on the list, where other fans who don't know about you yet will discover you.

20) Make Compelling Offers and Ask for the Sale

Some people make a purchase right away when something interests them. Some rarely make a purchase. And a lot of people teeter on the fence, not sure which direction to go. For this third group of good folks, you need to create incentives – reasons for them to hit the Buy button now. Here are some compelling possibilities:

- **Limited-time discounts**: Get a 20 percent discount if you purchase by this Friday.
- **Limited-quantity offers**: The first 25 people who respond get an autographed copy.
- **Upsell with a special offer**: Buy one, get one free. Or buy our new CD, get our previous release at half off.
- **Bundling**: Purchase a CD, T-shirt and cap at the same time, save 50 percent.
- **Charity benefit**: 20 percent of all CD sales proceeds go to the local Wildlife Refuge.

21) Boost Your CD Sales Without Lowering Your Price

Here's a great tip from Mike Barry, a New Zealand musician who plays in the rock band Fourth Member (www.fourthmember.com).

"We were playing a festival recently and had our CDs at the merchandise table along with two other bands," Mike writes, "but none of us was selling any." All three bands had their CDs on sale for $10 each. "Out of desperation, I made three piles of CDs and created a sign that read 'Festival Special! 3 CDs for $30.'"

The result? "We sold all three piles in 10 minutes! So we made three more piles and sold them in 10 minutes too. Before we knew it, there was a small crowd around the table. Just the thought of three CDs for $30 sounded too good to pass up. But what's funny is, that is how much it would have cost if the fans bought one off each of us to start with. Amazing!"

Mike's story reminds me of a lesson I learned at a retail store job I had when I was a teenager. I remember a manager one time bragging about how he took some trinket that sold for 39 cents each and sold out of them by displaying them with a sign that announced "2 for a dollar." Yes, the store sold more of them at a higher price. Why? Because the sign and display created a perception of value. Think about that ... and use this knowledge to sell more of your CDs and merchandise.

RESOURCES FOR MUSIC SALES AND DISTRIBUTION

22) CD Baby

www.cdbaby.com and www.cdbaby.net

Derek Sivers is one of the master marketers of the indie music world. His CD Baby site was one of the early online sources for new music. His staff is renowned for customer service and the speed at which they fill orders. Here's the scoop: For a one-time $35 setup fee, they scan your CD cover, convert your songs into streaming sound files, and create a unique web page for you on the site.

You set your selling price on CD Baby. They keep $4 per CD sold and pay you every week. CD Baby gives you every buyer's complete contact info, so you can do follow-up promotions and add them to your mailing list. Sales and inventory statistics are posted on the site.

Contact: CD Baby, 5925 NE 80th Ave., Portland, OR 97218. Phone: (503) 595-3000. E-mail: cdbaby@cdbaby.com.

23) Amazon.com

www.amazon.com/exec/obidos/subst/partners/direct/advantage-for-music.html

Sell your CDs along side major label releases. To be eligible for Amazon's Advantage program, each CD you want to enroll must have a UPC code printed or stickered on the cover. You must also own the distribution rights for your CD, be located in North America (U.S., Canada, or Mexico), and have an e-mail address and Web access. And you must be willing to part with 55 percent of your retail price. Millions of people shop at Amazon, so it's worth having a presence there.

24) The Home Grown Music Network

www.homegrownmusic.net

Founded in 1995 by Lee Crumpton of LEEWAY Productions, the Home Grown Music Network helps independent bands reach fans who are seeking fun, interesting and mind-expanding music. "We find the hottest touring bands – then turn fans on to them," says Crumpton. "The bands we seek are those who are breaking past existing boundaries and creating their own musical genres."

Contact: Leeway's HGMN, P.O. Box 340, Mebane, NC 27302. Phone: (919) 563 4923. E-mail: leeway@homegrownmusic.net.

25) Music Design

www.musicdesign.com

Music Design is a company that distributes a huge selection of contemporary instrumental New Age, Celtic, Native American, world, classical, jazz, folk and children's music. Music Design's niche is getting its CDs into "non-traditional music outlets," such as New Age shops, nature stores and gift shops.

The company mostly carries releases from established artists and labels, but will consider independent acts that fit into one of the above genres. Contact: Music Design, 4650 North Port Washington Rd., Milwaukee, WI 53212. Phone: (414) 961-8380.

26) Miles of Music

www.milesofmusic.com

"We here at MoM specialize in independently and self-released music," says the Miles of Music web site. "Our tastes are fairly wide ranged considering we're a bunch of old punk rockers and traditional country fans. We prefer full-length CDs, the more recently released the better, but we will consider all submissions. Other places take everything submitted or will charge you for inclusion. Not us! We take a select few in order to build an interesting and well-rounded catalog to offer our customers."

Contact: Miles of Music, 7306 Coldwater Canyon, Suite 9, North Hollywood, CA 91605. Phone: (818) 765-8836. E-mail: rune@milesofmusic.com.

27) Backroads Music and the Heartbeats Catalog

www.backroadsmusic.com

Backroads Music is a comprehensive source for ambient, space, world, new age, electronic, Celtic, Native American, guitar, piano and select vocal music. "We love indie labels," says owner Lloyd Barde, who explains that the company is not a wholesaler. "Backroads is strictly a mail order and fulfillment house." The company offers over 5,000 titles and publishes the *Heartbeats* catalog, which is sent to 60,000 subscribers.

Backroads also offers an toll-free ordering fulfillment service used my many record labels. If your music falls into the categories listed above, contact: Lloyd Barde, Backroads Music, 401-A Tamal Plaza, Corte Madera, CA 94925. Phone: (415) 924-4848. E-mail: mail@backroadsmusic.com.

28) Creative Musicians Coalition / Music Discoveries

www.aimcmc.com and www.musicdiscoveries.com

The Creative Musicians Coalition (CMC) is an international organization dedicated to the advancement of new music and the success of independent musicians. CMC represents more than 500 artists from 22 countries.

Music Discoveries is CMC's showcase site that brings music lovers, artists, the media and the industry closer together. The organization's mission is to encourage the exploration and discovery of new music generally hidden from the mainstream.

While many of CMC's are electronic and New Age-type artists, the coalition is open to all styles of music. Contact: Ronald Wallace, P.O. Box 6205, Peoria, IL 61601. Phone: (309) 685-4843. E-mail: aimcmc@aol.com.

29) Amazing CDs
www.amazingcds.com

This site is working hard to live up to its name. Right off the bat, Amazing CDs' home page announces, "Independent music artists' CDs from around the world – Listen and buy what you like right here!" There is a $25 set-up fee per CD submitted. Here's what you get: scanned cover art, artist page linked to your site, 60-second audio clips, artist profile and contact info. The site keeps a $3 commission per CD sold.

Amazing CDs also has a weekly CD Giveaway Sweepstakes – participating bands are encouraged to provide free discs for this promotion. Contact: Amazing CDs, 413 187th Street East, Dept 616, Spanaway, WA 98387. E-mail: info@amazingcds.com.

30) Homemade Music
www.homemademusic.com

This site is an offshoot of Bryan Baker's (no relation) long-standing *Gajoob* magazine. Tons of resources for indie bands, plus they can sell your CDs from the web site. Contact: Homemade Music, 1478 Stetson Circle, Salt Lake City, UT 84104. Phone: (800) 799-3010. E-mail: info@homemademusic.com.

31) eFolkMusic
www.efolkmusic.org

If you record and sell folk, bluegrass, Celtic music and the like, you should take a look at eFolkMusic. For a one-time $50 fee, the site can help you sell CDs, earn cash for single downloads and market your free downloadable music files. The coolest thing about eFolkMusic is that artists get the e-mail address of every fan who downloads their freebie MP3 files. Worth a look. Contact: eFolkMusic, 101 Evans Ct., Carrboro, NC 27510. Phone: (888) 376-3011. E-mail: info@efolkmusic.org.

32) The Orchard
www.theorchard.com

This site describes itself as "the largest distributor of independent music in the world." The Orchard allows you to sell your music using the same digital and physical distribution channels used by the major labels, including traditional retail outlets and Internet retail stores. Fees start at $49 per release. Contact: The Orchard, 133 5th Avenue, 7th Floor, New York, NY 10003. Phone: (212) 529-9109. E-mail: info@theorchard.com.

33) Planet CD Independent Music Store

www.planetcd.com

This site's home page reads, "Planet CD has been selling the best independent music since 1997. We provide artists an outlet to promote and sell their music. Learn about each artist, listen to their music. If you enjoy what you hear, show your support and purchase a CD!" There's a one-time set-up fee of $45 plus a $4 commission for every CD sold. Contact: Planet CD, P.O. Box 19481, Charlotte, NC 28219. Phone: (704) 560-2379. E-mail: info@planetcd.com.

34) Accept Payments from Your Own Web Site

You already know your fans can order your CDs securely online when you get set up with CD Baby, Amazon and some of the other sites listed here. But what if you want to take orders right from your own site? And what if you want to sell T-shirts, caps and other merchandise? Most of these sales outlets can't help you there. Here are four alternate payment processing services to consider using:

PayPal.com
www.paypal.com

2CheckOut.com
www.2checkout.com

CCnow.com
www.ccnow.com

Look over fees and policies carefully. Most charge a per-transaction fee plus a percentage of each sale. PayPal has the lowest fees and most flexible access to your money. But look them all over and see what works for you.

35) Research More Music Sales Outlets Online

Pay a visit to the **Google Directory** at http://directory.google.com and follow this path: Shopping > Entertainment > Recordings > Audio > Music > Specialty > Independent Artists. There you'll find a long list of additional music sales sources.

To sum up: Open your mind to the music sales possibilities all around you ... and you may soon find yourself with a lot of extra closet space.

Chapter 9

Why Your Local Music Scene Sucks (or How to Use the Power of Optimism to Turbo-charge Your Music Career)

The best way to start discussing this crucial topic is to relate something that happened a few years ago. Due to cramped quarters and a growing staff, I moved my business into a larger office space. With the new office came the need for a new telephone system. So a phone company rep came by to pitch what she had to offer.

During the conversation, of course, I let her know that I published *Spotlight*, my former music magazine. Unfortunately for her, she was not familiar with it. So I explained what the paper was and sent her off with a few copies to take home. About a week later she called to follow up and mentioned something I've heard many times over the years.

"You know, since I met you and learned more about *Spotlight*, I've seen the paper all over the place," she admitted. "I guess since I wasn't that aware of it before, I never noticed it sitting at all those locations."

This sales rep was guilty of a trait that's common among all human beings: being limited in her view of the world by what she chooses to focus on. It's no crime. We all carry these limited perceptions with us all the time.

Have you ever bought a new car and suddenly started seeing the same make and model everywhere you went? What caused that? Was there a sudden swell in sales of your type of car? Had you unknowingly started a fashion trend?

Not likely. The real reason is that you had a new awareness of that particular car style and your mind tuned in to those shapes and sizes.

Well, I contend that if your mind works that way with newspapers, cars, shapes and sizes, it also works that way with your attitudes, beliefs and expectations. Your mind seeks out what you choose to focus on.

Therefore, if you're one of those doom-and-gloom people who consistently tells yourself and others how much your local music scene sucks, I guarantee you'll see one example after another to support your limited (and limiting) belief.

Every time a club owner doesn't hire your band, a radio disc jockey doesn't play your song or a music editor doesn't assign a writer to cover you, you'll say, "See, what did I tell you? This town blows! Nobody cares about my music. There are no opportunities here. Why bother?"

So what's the solution?

Optimism. Pure and simple, developing a positive attitude and sense of optimism will do more for your music career advancement than the most expensive piece of new equipment or the most powerful industry big shot could do in a lifetime.

So stop whining and start considering these ideas to help you stretch and build your optimism muscles.

Develop balanced expectations

First off, you want to go into every situation expecting to get positive results. If you expect to win, your chances of getting what you want greatly increase. But taking this concept too far can backfire.

"I've met so many musicians who go into the music business expecting that things are going to be handed to them," says Ellen Persyn, lead vocalist for the band Radio Iodine. "And when they can't just walk into the most popular club in town and get a Saturday night headlining gig, they're so disillusioned that they get a really bad attitude."

Persyn moved from Philadelphia to St. Louis several years ago. She put together a new band that, in a relatively short time, became one of the top alternative/original music groups in St. Louis. Radio Iodine was eventually signed to Radioactive/MCA Records.

She thinks aspiring musicians should stay positive but not expect too much too soon. "Musicians get this narrow, little viewpoint that they're artists only," Persyn says. "They don't try to understand music from a business point of view, which can cause them to get really pessimistic."

Focus on the positive – but don't fake happiness

Russ Hopkins runs a project studio called Kiva Recording out of his home in Fort Collins, CO. He feels that maintaining a sense of optimism has helped his business and his hometown improve.

"I feel that Fort Collins is a unique environment and has a good music scene, but it's growing because people want it to grow and care about it," Hopkins says. "You can make optimism work by trying to see the positive, by supporting other musicians and always believing that anything can happen. And why not here? It takes people really looking and trying to see the good."

Hopkins has been one of the more visible supporters of music in his community, having produced two compilation CDs showcasing Fort Collins artists. But is his city free from negative thinking?

"On that level, I don't think this scene is any different," says Hopkins, who believes you shouldn't let the naysayers distract you from your goals. "I feel we have a lot of creative people in this city. I was just one of the first people to really champion that here and bring people's attention to it."

While affirming the positive, Persyn also suggests you know where to draw the line: "I don't view optimism as, 'Oh, I've got to put on a happy face and pretend that everything's going to be great.' This business is really hard. There are a lot of ups and downs.

"The way I maintain my optimism is taking it one step at a time, setting goals that are realistic and trying to see things from the other person's point of view," she says.

Embrace the work

Many aspiring artists psych themselves up with big expectations for a musical career but don't consider the work it takes to actually get there.

"There are always guys who walk up to me after our shows and say, 'This scene sucks but we want to open for you.' I'll say, 'Okay, send me a tape,' and they never send one. So, yeah, the scene sucks for them," Persyn says.

"Some bands think they're going to set the scene on fire because they're so good. I don't care if they really are good, it takes more than that. Even if your CD is fabulous, it takes a lot of work to get people to listen and realize you really are fabulous.

"I've noticed something about pessimistic musicians," she continues. "They think that things are just going to happen for them because they exist. But they aren't willing to make the phone calls or send the mailings."

Enjoy small steps and small victories

"When we started out, if I could get an opening gig on a Wednesday night, that was cool," Persyn explains. "Then my next expectation was getting opening gigs on the weekend. Next, I wanted split bills on the weekend.

"That way, I was still working toward my long-term goals, but I wasn't crushed by trying to leap to that big goal in one mighty bound. Every little victory increased my determination and my optimism, because I had set goals that were attainable.

"The first three months you're out there, nobody wants to talk to you," she adds. "So the keys are planning, short-term goals and focusing on the small victories."

Hopkins says that same technique can work for an entire music community. "We have a little bit of local and regional success, and that always helps," he says, citing that Big Head Todd & the Monsters come from the Boulder/Denver area, about 50 miles away. "I remember seeing them play at a sports bar near the college in Fort Collins."

Hopkins also points out that certain members of the Subdudes (another band that has garnered national exposure) make their home in Fort Collins. "It goes to show that you can experience success no matter where you live," he concludes.

But this small-victories approach doesn't end there. Hopkins also applies it to Kiva Recording. "My optimism came about as a result of building my studio business and my confidence slowly," he says. "I used to think, 'If I can get clients with the primitive gear that I have, just imagine if I had a setup that allowed me to offer even more.'" After a couple of years, he was able to upgrade his equipment – just as he had imagined.

Set realistic goals

One of the worst things you can do is pursue a goal you have practically no chance of reaching. It's important to set your sights on something that will challenge and stretch your abilities but not overwhelm you. Also, break your big goals into small, manageable chunks, and make sure your short-term activities support your long-range plans.

"With us, we have long-term goals and six-month goals, then I have a goal for the next two weeks," says Persyn. "I make it a point every couple of months to sit down and review long-term what I want to do with my life."

See things from other people's points of view

"If you go into this business expecting that 'Everybody should promote me,' but you don't give back, you're going to face a tough battle ahead," continues Persyn, who prefers to adopt an attitude that allows her to work as a partner with the people who can help her band the most. That includes supplying music editors and writers with all the materials they need in a timely manner, collaborating with club owners on joint promotions, etc.

"I don't want a nightclub to suffer when we play there. I want them to do great," she adds. "Approach it from their point of view. What can you do for them?"

Hopkins, likewise, looks at his business from his customer's point of view, which he says includes being able to "record inexpensively, get CDs duplicated and other services that help artists get their music out on a local level cost effectively."

Before he opened his home studio to the public, Hopkins says there was one other recording facility in town. It had been there for some time and was successful, but the owner reportedly didn't rate very high in the customer-satisfaction department. "He was the only guy in town," recalls Hopkins. "I felt if he's doing as well as he's doing treating people that way, there must be a strong need for recording services."

Hopkins couldn't compete based on size and equipment but, by seeing things from the buyer's point of view, he was able to compete by offering more personalized service.

Avoid bitterness – don't take everything personally

"For me, and I'm still getting over this ... realize that other people have down times, too," Persyn offers. "Other bands fight to get gigs, work hard to build a following and have bad nights. So when those things happen to you, you can't let it crush you and turn you bitter. No one's going to hand you anything, but at the same time everybody goes through these things and you have to roll with the punches.

"I believe there are up times and down times for everybody. Nobody questions it when things are going great. I didn't say, 'Oh God, why me?' when we had 400 people at our CD release party.

"However, my first reaction when we have a small crowd at a show is pessimism: 'Oh man, this is bad, I should just give up.' A bad draw just devastates me. I'm depressed for three days. I don't understand why it happened," she says.

"I'm not saying I don't get down and think about chucking the whole thing. This business takes so much work. But if I hang in there, things will spring back around. And that's exactly what has always happened."

Plant seeds

Persyn offers more timeless advice on planning for the future: "Another thing I do to cope is something I call seed planting. If you just sit on your butt and you don't send out any demo tapes or make contacts or phone calls, then in three months you're not going to have anything to harvest. It's only by putting out those seeds that you can look forward to some fruit in two to three months."

Keep the faith

"I've definitely created a niche for myself here that so far is working," says Hopkins. "Part of that comes from my faith." But the faith he refers to isn't necessarily in a religious context. It stems from the power that any human being can tap – the power that comes from believing in yourself and your ability to make positive things happen.

"Faith is more of an attitude," he explains. "You can say, 'We're at this level and it can only get worse.' Or you can say, 'We're at this level and it can only get better.' It could get better or worse – but maybe we can have something to say about which direction we actually take."

Tap into your passion

While succeeding monetarily and otherwise is a goal toward which most music people strive, optimism will be a lot easier to maintain if you're pursuing a line of work (and play) that truly excites you.

"For years I wasn't really worried about making money," says Hopkins of his recording activities. "I just wanted to do it and gain the experience. And that was a fairly conscious decision. But the more I submerged myself in it and the more experience I got, the more paying customers I ended up having."

Persyn wraps things up with a similar sentiment. "I guess optimism for me comes down to this: I really do believe in our music and I'm willing to do the work on each small step to make it happen," she says. "And that's better than lying in bed, depressed all the time."

Chapter 10

25 Creative Ways to Finance Your Next Recording Project, Music Video or Major Equipment Purchase

You've heard the expression "It takes money to make money." And sometimes it does. You've also heard horror stories about the complications of bank loans, business plans, lawyers and meddling investors. And it's those negative mental associations that keep many aspiring music people from ever taking a stab at a big project – whether it's committing to a CD release, buying a new sound and lighting system, producing a music video or starting a small record label.

I can hear you now: "Man, I'm never going to be able to get a bank loan. And I wouldn't trust a power-hungry investor with my career. Why bother?" Well, I say don't let those perceived obstacles stop you from getting what you want!

For now let's forget about bank loans and high finance – although we will touch on them briefly a little later. Instead, let's think about more creative, street-level methods of raising money. Let's call it Guerrilla Music Financing, because we're going to be attacking this money-raising business from the ground level, where we can get a lot more accomplished by relying on our creativity.

Important Note: The first rule of Guerrilla Music Financing to grasp is that – unlike the traditional road to investment capital, where a large lump sum of money comes from one almighty source – we guerrillas have to think in terms of combining a number of smaller money-raising streams into one sizable river of cash.

What follows is a list of 25 specific actions you can take now to get money flowing toward your musical project.

Six ways to raise thousands of dollars yourself

This next statement might seem obvious, but it's important to note: Your best source for funding your musical projects is *you*. By taking control of your own financing, you avoid having to answer to a co-signer or investor. The feeling of freedom alone will lighten the load of small sacrifices you may have to make along the way.

Here are six great ways to turn to yourself for money matters:

• Set aside a percentage of your day job salary

First, set up a special savings account at your bank for the exclusive purpose of building a Guerrilla Music Project Fund. Setting aside just $25 a week will give you about $650 in only six months. And while your money is growing and earning interest at the bank, you can use this time to scout around for the best possible deal on studio time, video production, sound systems or whatever it is you'll be investing in.

• Earn extra cash to stash for your project

Humans have an uncanny ability to get things done when they are truly motivated. Don't limit yourself by thinking within the confines of your present financial situation. Could you possibly earn extra money by giving guitar lessons, working as a studio session player or as a solo act?

There are dozens of ways for people in the music business to make extra cash with their talents. Don't be a victim of tunnel vision. Playing a paid gig is just one of many ways to profit from music. Do you have skills at home recording, publicity, web site design or even running sound and lights for other bands? Use your creativity.

Note: Earning an additional $25 a week would give you another $650 in six months – a total of $1,300!

• Sell your old equipment

Most musicians have at least some seldom-used equipment sitting around in the basement or garage. Some have quite a bit. Is there a good reason why you continue to hang on to it? If not, you may be cheating yourself out of the extra cash you could make by selling it.

Run a classified ad or post notices at music stores in your area. Blow the dust off some of those old suckers, sell them and add some money to your Guerrilla Music Project Fund.

Another Possibility: Many used CD stores pay cash for decent pre-owned releases. Use your head and cash in on stuff you already have!

- ## Spend less on other gear – buy only what you need

The main point here is to be realistic. Just as you define your musical and creative needs, you should also assess your technical and production needs. Separate what you would like to have from what you actually need.

Do you really require that 24-channel board when a 16-channel mixer would do the job for a lot less money? Is that $500 guitar effects rack something you really need? Or is advertising your new release in a national magazine really necessary, when you may be better off promoting it on a regional level, where it will have more impact and cost less?

- ## Get a bank loan or line of credit

If you have a good credit rating, you have the option of getting a bank loan. True, this is what you want to avoid if you truly embrace the "guerrilla" philosophy. But some musicians are more financially secure than others. If you have some monetary stability and are confident about your future in music – at least for the next couple of years – this is a tempting option. Just make sure you don't strap yourself with loan payments if the band breaks up or CD sales aren't as brisk as you hoped.

Note: There are plenty of juicy guerrilla suggestions still to come in this chapter, and many of them will be even better, less-costly ways to go about getting the funds you want.

- ## Use credit cards

Another method of financing is using a credit card. This is basically a loan, but I listed it separately because many people overlook it as a financing option. You can either purchase items directly by charging them to the card or get a lump sum cash advance to spend on a variety of things.

Credit cards carry the same disadvantages of a loan, only those low minimum payments make the dangers of snowballing interest even greater. However, life is often a gamble and a lot of musicians have used credit cards to fund everything from PA and lighting purchases to entire CD releases.

I'll never forget the time I received a promotional mailing from a West Coast artist. The flier read, "Sponsored by Visa, MasterCard and American Express" – pointing out, in a humorous way, that he was an independent artist funding his CD project with his personal credit cards. It certainly caught my eye, and it definitely helped him get his music out into the world. So keep credit cards in mind, but use them cautiously.

Two more ways to raise money fast

• Solicit family members and friends

If you still need more funds after putting to use all the possibilities of raising cash yourself, the next safest bets are family members and friends. While borrowing money from relatives and acquaintances is a natural for some people, it can be a stomach-churning curse for others. So move slowly in this area.

Even though these casual investors are fronting you money because they care for and believe in you, you'd be wise to spell out everything on paper before accepting any friendly funding. Get it all in writing. Will you have to pay it back, and if so, when? How much input will Aunt Gertrude want on your next album if she's footing the bill? Find out ahead of time and you'll keep everyone happy.

• Seek out investors

Now we move into a more complicated realm. To attract investors you usually have to come up with a written business plan that includes budgets, expenses, projected revenues and countless other tedious details. If you're uncomfortable with numbers, fine print and selling yourself, traditional investment strategies might not work for you.

Most musical acts that attract investors basically end up making fans of people who have extra money to play with. In other words, investors should ideally have their hearts into what your music and vibe are all about.

Question: How do you find supportive investors? By being sociable and meeting all of your fans. It's that simple. Plus, don't be shy about mentioning to people that you're looking for an investor (or two, or five). In fact, many artists have found it's easier to find 10 people who each invest $1,000 than it is to search for one person who can invest the whole $10,000.

When you find interested parties, you must demonstrate that you and your music have merit and potential to make money for both you and the investor. Along with a business plan that spells out everything about your music career, clip articles from respected magazines on similar success stories and highlight industry trends based on information from trade publications. Also, it doesn't hurt to list a respected person in the music industry as your personal consultant.

Agree ahead of time on what role the investor will play in your career. Will he or she be hands-on or more of a silent partner? Will the investor be reimbursed through an ongoing percentage of your earnings or only at a specific time, such as when your band gets signed to a record deal? Make sure the details are clear and beneficial to both parties, and have an attorney look over the final agreement.

Four more ways to get the financing you need

• Use your personal credit

Okay, so you don't have the financial clout to get a mega-bucks bank loan. Does that mean you're completely out of luck when it comes to getting credit? Maybe not.

Is there a music store, recording studio or video producer in town who you've developed a good relationship with? If so, don't overlook the good possibility of getting personal credit from the owner of one of these establishments. This arrangement is basically an informal loan. The business owner, in essence, would front you the equipment, studio time or service for now ... with the understanding that you will pay the fee at a future date when you're able. As always, be specific on the repayment timetable and dollar amounts.

• Offer sponsorships

Coke, Pepsi, Miller Genuine Draft and Bud Light aren't the only brand names that can sponsor musical events. Even though the corporate big guys are best known for it, why couldn't your local music store or studio sponsor you? You put up posters and pass out fliers promoting their businesses at your shows ... and they give you a discount or free stuff in exchange. What a concept!

• Practice the ancient art of barter

Do you have a skill, product or service that would be of value to a recording studio owner, video producer, newspaper publisher or CD replicater? Well, if they have something you want, and you have something they want, it may be time to put the ancient art of trading goods and services into action. That's what bartering is all about, and it works perfectly for Guerrilla Music Financing. In fact, it may be one of your most powerful tactics for financing your music venture on a limited budget.

Another Angle: What if the business owner isn't interested in what you can offer? You're next option would be what I call a Trade Triangle. Ask the owner what he'd be willing to barter for if there were no limits. Let's say a studio owner needs a new transmission on his car. Perhaps you know (or can find) a mechanic who might be interested in what you have to offer – maybe your band could play free at the company's upcoming anniversary street party.

Then you create a Trade Triangle. The mechanic gets free entertainment from you, the studio guy gets a new transmission, and you get your free recording time from the studio. Everybody's happy ... and without spending a dime! That's Guerrilla Music Financing at its best.

• Build your own equipment

That's right, you read that correctly. Why buy a new, expensive sound system or effects rack when you might be able to build one yourself for a lot less cash? If you have carpentry skills and a working knowledge of acoustics and electronics, this could be a real money-saving method for you ... whether you're building a sound system or home recording studio. Here are several good build-your-own electronic equipment resources:

Midwest Analog Products
www.midwest-analog.com

PAiA Electronics
www.paia.com
paia@paia.com
(405) 340-6300

Digi-Key
www.digikey.com
(800) 344-4539

Guitar Effects Web Page
www.geofex.com

Music Electronic Archive
http://audible.transient.net/archive/

Three great ways to create cash if you're in a working band

• Save money from paying jobs

One of the best ways for a working band to raise a lot of cash for a major project is through paying gigs. Even a band that works part-time could easily come up with at least $500 a month from live shows – that's another $3,000 for your Guerrilla Music Project Fund in six months.

This method is a lot easier to manage, though, if the members don't depend on band job money for basic living expenses. If the members really need the steady cash, try setting aside a percentage of gig money from each job, even if it's only 10 to 20 percent. Just take it off the top before everyone gets paid.

• Promote fund-raising gigs

Non-profit companies, environmental coalitions and charities of all types use fund-raising events to come up with the operating cash for their organizations. People generally like to do something constructive for a good cause, so they show up and donate money. Well, if this technique works for charities, it can also work for your musical act's fund-raising needs.

Strategy: Pick a night when you're booked at a local club or hall and promote it as a "Show Your Support Night." Ask your fans to play a part in your success story by helping you fund your next CD. Charge a minimum $10 donation at the door. Let attendees know that all the proceeds collected that night go toward financing the recording. Maybe even offer to list everyone's name in the CD credits if they contribute.

You could also use this event to pre-sell your CDs – in effect, earning revenue before you've even produced them. Remember, you won't get things in life unless you ask for them. Just make sure to give something of value back in return.

• Sell CDs, tapes, T-Shirts and merchandise

Your live shows can bring in a lot more money than just your performance fee or what you collect at the door in cover charges. If you and your act aren't taking full advantage of merchandising, you're missing the financial boat. Bands with even modest followings are reaping lots of extra money by selling T-shirts, caps, buttons, stickers and more.

Obviously, if you're trying to raise money for a recording project, you may not have a CD or tape to sell. But if you do, by all means, push them doggies at your live shows. Mentioning them often and enthusiastically from the stage is a good start. But if you really want to cash in on merchandising, set up a booth or table chock full of everything you have to sell and make sure a friend, roadie or associate mans it the entire night.

Important Note: If you're seriously using fund-raising and merchandising as a means to finance your next musical project, you'd be wise to take all the money earned through these methods and put it directly into your Guerrilla Music Project Fund account. And don't touch it until you're ready to invest in your specific project.

So you think this idea of raising cash from gig money and merchandising is great. But wait! What if your goal is to purchase a PA and light show? Without them, you can't play out to earn money. And without that extra money, you'll never be able to afford them. It's the ultimate Catch 22, right? *Wrong!* Here are some solid ways to play out and make money without your own system.

(*Note:* These next three suggestions might seem elementary, but I include them just in case you're overlooking them.)

• Work at clubs that have house systems

More and more nightclub venues have their own in-house sound and lighting systems. By providing them, club owners can get bands to play for lower rates, since the band doesn't have to haul in and set up its own system. Your job, then, is to find the clubs in your area with house systems and try to get work in those venues first. By doing so, you'll get those paid jobs and merchandising opportunities – without needing your own PA and lights.

• Work with bands that have systems

While you're looking at venues with house systems, don't overlook other opportunities for paid work at other clubs. One way is to work with other bands that already have good sound and lighting systems. Whether you're opening, doing a split bill or headlining, try to align yourself with groups that will allow you to use their systems at shared gigs.

You may have to help cover the cost of the soundman or roadies, or even do a little roadie work yourself. But that's a small price to pay, considering the other band is bringing in what you don't have. By using this arrangement, you'll open up your moneymaking possibilities to include practically any venue in your region.

• Rent from stores, bands or discount sound and lighting services

This may be another selection from the Overly Obvious category, but here it is anyway: When you have a paid gig beckoning and you don't have a sound or lighting system of your own, renting one or hiring someone to bring one in might be your best solution – especially if you know you'll earn more than you'll spend on the show.

Your options include renting PA and lights from music stores, sound companies or other bands and running them yourself. But don't forget about hiring a freelancer to come in and do all the dirty work for you … at a higher price, of course. Some of the best deals may come from other bands that rent systems on their nights off (in fact, they may be doing it to build their own Guerrilla Music Project Funds).

Adding it all up

Let's figure out what a four-piece band might be able to raise in six months using just some of the techniques listed here. First, let's start with your potential as an individual. Suppose you were able to set aside just $20 a week from your "real job" for your Guerrilla Music Project Fund. You'd have just over $500 in six months. Then suppose you could earn an additional $20 a week giving lessons, doing home recording or any number of things discussed earlier. That would give you another $500.

If you really tried, you could probably raise about $250 selling off some old equipment. And by trimming back some of your more extravagant musical expenses, you should be able to redirect another $250 into the account over the six-month period. That gives you a total of $1,500 in six months using only your own discipline and ingenuity.

Even though you could easily raise still more money by getting a credit card cash advance or a $500 to $1,000 loan from a family member, let's use the more conservative $1,500 individual figure for our purposes. Now multiply that number by the four people in our four-member example band. Suddenly we've got $6,000 in the collective Guerrilla Music Project Fund.

And we haven't even factored in fund-raising gigs, paid band jobs and merchandise sales. Over the course of six months, a band could easily raise another $3,000 from these sources. Add that to the previous subtotal and you'd be on your way to raising nearly $10,000 for your next project!

10 ways to get a better price when buying equipment

You've heard the saying: A penny saved is a penny earned. It's true. Don't spend more than you have to on equipment. Use these tips and save.

• Buy used gear

Finding good, pre-owned equipment can suit your needs and be a lot easier on your pocketbook at the same time. Shop around and test the stuff before you buy.

• Shop by mail order

Ordering gear by mail can often get you lower prices while allowing you to avoid paying in-state sales tax. Here are three good mail order equipment sources:

Musician's Friend
www.musiciansfriend.com
(800) 776-5173

Carvin
www.carvin.com
(800) 854-2235

• Pay cash up front

No secret here. If you've done a good job of setting aside money for your Guerrilla Music Project Fund, walking into a store or studio with cash in hand will always give you plenty of leverage to get a great, low price.

• Compare prices and shop around

I don't mean to insult your intelligence here, but too often many of us get hooked on the first offer we come across ... and quite often it's not the best buy. Resist impulse buying and check out other options before you commit.

• Establish a relationship with one retailer or studio

On the other end of the spectrum from shopping around is being loyal to one business ... that is, if it rewards you for your patronage with lower prices. If you've done a noticeable amount of business with one particular music dealer in town, ask about a preferred customer discount.

• Consider display models

Ranking right up there with used equipment bargains is the super price you can often get on demo models. Eventually, stores have to dispose of the display units that sit on the sales floor. And they move them by letting somebody walk out with these items at a 30- to 70-percent discount. That somebody might as well be you!

• Take advantage of sales, liquidations and going out of business specials

Keeping an ear to your regional music grapevine might help alert you when a retailer is going out of business. When this occurs, you can bet the business owner will be more than eager to sell remaining equipment at deep discounts.

• Buy at wholesale by helping a store meet its quota

When music stores buy equipment from suppliers, the discount they get depends on the total amount of gear the store purchases. The higher the dollar amount, the better the wholesale price. Knowing this, why not offer to buy that monster PA system from the store at wholesale cost, which might help the store up its purchasing power and get a bigger discount from its supplier? It's worth a shot.

- ## Work at a music store

Sure, why not? As an employee, you'll probably get a discount on any purchase you make while you work for the store. Plus you'll get a paycheck from the store! Yet another option.

- ## Haggle ... and ask for a better price!

This one was added because too many people simply forget to do it. The number listed on the price tag is, more often than not, negotiable. And if you never ask for a lower price, it certainly won't be offered to you. So ask ... and you just might receive a great price break.

Congratulations! You've made it through all 25 creative ways to finance your next music project. What you need to do now is go through the couple dozen moneymaking and money-saving suggestions in this report (by the way, feel free to add some of your own) and start deciding which methods are going to work best for you.

Some musicians have access to investors while others feel stronger about going the merchandising route. Some are in a better position to set aside cash from their regular jobs while others opt for a credit card advance.

Remember the river of Guerrilla Music Financing we covered at the beginning of this chapter? The best money-raising plan will incorporate several different streams. A little savings here, some extra revenue there ... it can all add up quickly.

Your new action plan

Finally, I'd like to talk about one of the most important aspects of raising money in the music business: setting weekly and monthly goals. Once you narrow down your financial plan of attack, put it on paper. Give yourself a specific amount of money you want to raise and a date by which you want to have the total in your Guerrilla Music Project Fund.

Then make sure and open a separate bank account for this special fund. I suggest using at least a six-month plan and being realistic about the dollar amounts. Setting unattainable goals will do nothing but wear down your confidence in reaching them.

Next, break up the dollar amounts into monthly and weekly figures. In other words, calculate how much you're going to have to earn or set aside each week in specific categories to hit your target amount. Breaking it up into bite-size chunks makes any worthy goal more manageable and keeps you on track week after week in your pursuit of it.

When it comes to sponsorships, bartering and other less-tangible methods, write out your specific action plan: who you'll contact, when you'll make contact, what offer will be made, etc. Once these steps are taken and a response is received, it's time to reevaluate the plan. Just as an airplane pilot readjusts his flight pattern many times before reaching a specific destination, so should you adjust your financial action plan along the way to reaching your money goals.

Bottom Line: The choice is now yours. If you don't consider all the money-raising possibilities and write out a plan to begin with, you'll continue to stray (like so many people) down a wandering path to musical obscurity. Not creating your personal road map and being committed to it week after week, month after month, will lead you only to *not* getting that new release out, *not* getting that music video produced or *not* getting that killer sound system you need.

But since you now have more than two dozen solid ideas at your fingertips and the newfound commitment to reach your financial and creative goals, you'll be one of the smart ones basking in the glow of having attained yet another one of your musical dreams.

Chapter 11

How to Use the Telephone More Effectively to Get Paying Gigs, Radio Airplay and Press Coverage

No doubt about it, the telephone is still one of the most powerful tools you can use to turbo-charge your career in the music business. Even with modern communications alternatives such as e-mail, text messaging and video conferencing, the phone is still the workhorse of methods available to promote your music.

This leads to some good news and bad news concerning all this business of dialing for dollars (and exposure). First, the bad news: Virtually everyone has a telephone, which means that millions of people are already using the phone to compete with you in your quest to get media coverage, airplay, paying gigs and record sales.

Now the good news: While all of these people are cluttering the phone lines with their own messages, many of them are using weak and destructive tactics with Mr. Bell's fine invention. This sets the stage for people who know the tricks and nuances of telephone marketing to get ahead by using it effectively.

I've lost track of the times I've received calls from poor, misdirected fools who open a conversation with, "Hello, is this Bob Barker?" My response: "No, he's the game show host, but I do encourage you to have your cats and dogs spayed and neutered."

Then there was the caller who once asked my office manager, "What issue of the *Riverfront Times* [a competing newspaper in town] will my CD review run in?" Her response: "Why don't you call them to find out?"

Can you see how this rampant and mindless abuse of the phone can work against so many people? And how easy it would be to stand out from the pack and get more of what you want by doing your homework and using a few simple telephone marketing tips?

Start putting the following suggestions to use in your music promotion efforts and you won't have to worry about calling anyone a game show host again.

Go through a mini-rehearsal before making your next call

In the same way that your band sounds a lot less polished when you haven't been practicing, so will your telephone presentation be rusty if you haven't prepared beforehand.

Solution: Simply take a minute before each call and consider what your objective is and the approach you'll use. When calling on a nightclub owner, stumbling around with vague phrases such as "Um, hey, you don't know me but ... uh, I play in a band ... and I was wondering what it would take to get my band to play your club ..." won't get you any closer to that gig.

What will help is identifying your objective: trying to get an opening slot for a specific band, wanting to establish a relationship with the owner, persuading the owner to set aside a night to hold a benefit concert, etc. Also, plan what approach you'll take: mentioning mutual friends and the recommendations they've given, offering to drop by at a convenient time to meet with the owner for 10 minutes, having a list of bands who've agreed to play a benefit and so on.

Choose one specific objective and one approach before you make each phone call.

Number your points for impact

Whether you're calling a newspaper editor to get a story or a nightclub owner to get a paying gig, consider using a number to indicate how many important points you plan to touch on.

Example: "Pat, I know you have a lot of bands that want press in your paper (or want to work at your club), but I'd like to mention three benefits you'd get from using us ..." People will listen more attentively when they know how many points they will hear – plus, it helps you organize your thoughts.

Give two positive choices when making your pitch

The worst thing you can do when marketing your music by phone is ask the other person to make a choice between "yes" and "no." In other words, if you were speaking with a radio station music director, it wouldn't be wise to say, "So, will you play my new single or not?" A question like that makes it too easy for the other person to say, "No."

Better: Instead, do a little research on the station's shows and disc jockeys. Then ask a question along the lines of, "Do you think this song would work better for you on Sarah's morning show or during Greg's new music show at night?" This way, you give the contact two choices – neither one of which is not playing your song.

If you were speaking with a music business attorney seeking representation, you might ask, "Would you like me to snail mail our CD and promo package to you today or e-mail a link to our electronic press kit?"

Apply this method to conversations with club owners, retailers and other media people, too.

Keep plugging away when you're on a roll

Let's be honest, there are times when we're "hot" and times we're "not." While we'd all like to be energetic and effective at all times (and there are ways to reach that productive state more often), sometimes it just doesn't happen. Therefore, take advantage of those times when you're on a roll by staying at it.

Let's say you just got off the phone with a club manager who finally booked your act into that long-awaited weekend headlining slot. You may be tempted to call your band mates and rejoice at the victory or sit for a while and dwell on your success.

Instead, pick up the phone and call another contact immediately. Strike while the music marketing iron is hot! Productivity has a funny way of multiplying when you're on a roll.

Use a music marketing log to stay on track

If you make even a minimal amount of phone calls to promote your music career, you know how easy it is to forget important details such as who you called, when you called them, what was discussed and how you were supposed to follow up.

What you want to avoid is calling someone and saying, "Hello, Bill. Say, didn't I talk to you last month about doing a feature story on my band? Or was it for your review column? ... Oh, that's right. Anyway, did you ever get our new CD? I'm pretty sure I sent it out to you ..."

Solution: Use a music marketing log sheet for each contact you call. Print a fill-in-the-blank form that includes lines for name, company, e-mail and street addresses, phone and fax numbers. Below that leave plenty of space for columns that list the date of contact, topics discussed, action you need to take next, and when you took that action.

Then print dozens of copies of the blank sheets and divide them in a three-ring binder into categories such as print media, radio, nightclubs, online music sites, record stores, distributors, etc. Start using these log sheets every time you communicate with someone about marketing your music, and jot down notes in the appropriate spaces.

Bottom line: By using these marketing logs, everything you need to know about any contact is listed on only one page. And the next time you call them you'll have the confidence to start the conversation by saying something like, "Hello, Bill. I was following up on the discussion we had two weeks ago concerning my band's new release. You mentioned you might have room for a review in your December issue. I mailed a CD to you on the 10th. Is there anything else I can do to help you make that review happen?"

Find out exactly what the contact wants

Most people who market their music by phone like to pile on layer after layer of self-congratulatory nonsense. They beat their chests and tell some innocent victim how much they like themselves, using an endless stream of adjectives. Meanwhile, the contact waits on the other end of the phone for a chance to break in and tell the caller what he or she really needs to know.

Even though I've had to endure countless calls like this over the years, please spare the people you call from this torturous ritual. Instead, make it your goal to find out what your contact needs from you to make what you want materialize. While you should speak of your project in positive terms, don't jump headlong into a dissertation on your great qualities before first finding out what it is your contact is looking for.

Example: You might talk a music editor's ear off about your alternative band's new CD. Little do you know, the editor just got out of a meeting in which the staff agreed they were covering too much local alternative music. What you also didn't know was that the editor was planning a story on band members with unique day jobs. Had you slowed down and asked a few questions, you might have discovered that. Then you could have let the editor know about your drummer, Phil, a parachute instructor.

Bottom line: It's always best to ask questions and find out what your contact's needs are. That way you'll open up a lot more opportunities for gigs, press and airplay – and get brushed off a lot less often.

Make sure you contact the right person

First, it should be a given that you uncover the names of the people who can help you (the proper editor, writer, music director, talent buyer, etc.) at the places you call. And if you get a name from a directory listing or through a suggestion from a friend, call the company and verify two things:

1) The person still works there and continues to hold the same title, and ...

2) You have the correct spelling and pronunciation of the person's name (recall the Bob Barker story I mentioned earlier).

In addition to that, it would help to investigate further and make sure the contact's duties truly relate to what you're going after. For instance, while I published my former music magazine, I carried the title of editor and publisher. And it's true that I made the final decisions on what subjects were covered in the paper. Therefore, people seeking publicity naturally tended to ask for me when they called.

What they quickly discovered – that is, if they used the right approach – was that the magazine's production manager, not me, was the person responsible for handling callers who pitched story ideas.

Too many of these eager, exposure-seeking individuals made the mistake of asking for me instead of explaining who they were and why they were calling. Consequently, these calls rarely, if ever, got returned. And the poor souls who placed them surely cursed the world and wondered why they were being cheated out of their share of publicity.

Lesson: Ask a couple of basic questions, explain your purpose for calling and find out if the name you have is really the best person to contact. People will help you out if you only let them.

Give honest compliments when appropriate

Use this one sparingly, because if it's not rendered with genuine appreciation, it could backfire. However, if you sincerely like the stand a writer took in a recent article, the new radio show a program director developed, or the remodeling a club owner just finished, tell them so.

This not only makes them feel good, but it shows them you're paying attention to what they're doing and are interested in more than just your own self-absorbed advancement.

Take the blame when the person doesn't understand what you're pitching

One thing you can count on is that there will be times when the contact on the other end of the line just doesn't comprehend your vision for a paid gig, a write-up, etc. Obviously, a bad move would be to condemn the person by barking, "Aren't you getting any of this?" or "Maybe if I speak slower you'll be able to keep up with me" (although you'll often be tempted to say just that).

At times like this, it's best to realize that the person might be distracted by something, is right in the middle of another project, or simply isn't up on the musical style or topic you're presenting. Remember, no one will be as interested in your music and career as much as you are.

Better approach: Be patient and offer positive remarks, such as:

- "Would there be a better time for me to call you back to talk about how my new single ended up in a movie soundtrack?" Or ...

- "I'm sorry, I must not be clearly explaining how my band could bring a few more people into your club."

Note that both of these statements include a benefit to the contact, as well as a polite way to clarify your pitch.

Grab their attention

Sometimes your contact's thoughts will wander. He or she simply won't be hanging on every word that comes out of your mouth during a phone conversation. One way to bring them back is to use an attention-getting statement. Here are a few good ones to try:

1) "Fran, if you don't remember anything else about my band, please note that ..."

2) "Jim, if I had to give you the number one reason to give this band airplay, it would be this ..."

3) "Mary, I've never told anybody this before, but ..."

4) "Joe, in addition to everything we've talked about, there's one overriding reason we should be playing your nightclub on weekends ..."

5) "You know, the best thing I could do for you right now is this ..."

Warning: If you're going to set someone up for a convincing, eye-opening revelation, make sure what you reveal packs a mean punch.

The final point-blank approach

There comes a time when you've done seemingly everything in your power to book the gig, make the appointment, get the airplay ... and still your phone contact waffles around with vague reasons for not giving you what you want – without firmly saying he or she isn't interested.

At this point, the direct approach is the best. Here are four last-resort techniques:

1) "So you're waiting for ... what ... before you go ahead with the story?"

2) "John, we already have this much invested in making this club date a reality, why not get out your calendar right now and schedule it?"

3) "I've given you everything you need to add this song into rotation. Can we please take the next step and make it happen?"

4) "Fred, I need your help. What will it take to get this done?"

Important note: Use these final approaches only after you've:

- Supplied the contact with everything he or she asked for
- Made at least a few initial contacts
- Been polite and professional throughout
- Pitched a number of specific ideas to help get what you want
- Kept the contact's interests foremost in mind

Otherwise, the person on the other end of the phone will think you're simply a pompous buffoon. And you wouldn't want that to happen, would you?

Yes, there is an important place for the telephone in your music promotion efforts. Use the ideas in this chapter to reach the right people, start meaningful relationships and get more of what you want in the music business.

Chapter 12

13 Low-Cost, High-Impact Music Promotion Ideas That Work

Recognition! Respect! A legion of loyal fans! Those are the rewards that most working musicians aspire to have. Yet, I've lost count of the number of frustrated artists I've encountered who work hard at their music but end up playing to empty rooms and accepting sluggish CD sales as a way of life.

Of course, you already know that any musical act must first have great songs, strong vocals, a defined musical identity and an engaging live show to have half a chance at making a splash with fans and industry people. Therefore, it's no surprise when bands that lack those elements don't cut it.

But how many times have you seen (or been in) a killer band and said to yourself, "This group really deserves to have a crowd. People don't know what they're missing"? More than a few times, right?

The problem with these bands is that they miss the big picture and concentrate almost entirely on the music – which is admirable, but it leaves the marketing aspects of their music to chance. Long ago, I made a decision that I wanted more control over my career. I no longer depend on the whims of fate to steer my life. I suggest you embrace the same attitude.

Bottom Line: Getting a grip on the promotional aspects of your music stacks the deck in your favor. Marketing helps you grab the attention of new fans and gets your music into their ears. Spending energy on creative promotional activities cranks your career into overdrive. When you market yourself effectively, you're able to spend more time making great music and less time rolling the dice and hoping a crowd shows up.

Another thing: Attention-getting tactics don't have to be complicated or expensive. You just have to think beyond simply pinning up fliers and letting some of your friends know about your gigs. Also, it's important to realize that no one promotional effort is going to work miracles. The low-budget, grass-roots music marketing approach that I advocate is a long-term, ongoing activity – not a one-shot deal.

Important Note: Music marketing is a lot like multi-track recording. Each layer you create adds to the layers already put down. That's why you need to develop and deploy an ongoing series of promotional assaults – with each one reaching more people and making them more familiar with your name, image and sound.

What follows is a list of 13 low-cost ideas you can use to promote your music. Hopefully, reading these methods will inspire you to not only use them, but to come up with even better marketing tactics of your own.

1) Hold a contest related to your band or release

Can you come up with a fresh idea to fire up the competitive spirit of music fans in your area? The band Symon Asher did. This Seattle, WA-based group held a contest to guess the origin of its name. To register, people had to visit local record stores and fill out an entry form. Clues on the band's name were mailed weekly to radio stations and the music press, creating even more of a buzz about the band.

Why It Works: There are five very effective angles to this promotional scheme:

- Forcing interested fans to register at record stores puts those contestants right smack in the middle of the record-buying environment, where they can easily listen to and buy your CD.

- By bringing more people into their shops, record store owners have more incentive to promote the contest in-house, giving you even more exposure to music consumers.

- Since the contest is about nothing but the band's name, the publicity benefit is priceless: name recognition!

- By hanging onto all the entry forms, you'll have a hefty batch of fresh names to add to your mailing list.

- Getting the media involved by sending them clues to give to their audiences adds yet another layer of exposure – one that most publicists would die for.

Find a way to make the contest idea work for your band. It could just as easily be applied to the title of a song or new release, too.

(By the way, if you're dying to know, the band mentioned above was named after the birth name of former Cream bassist/vocalist Jack Bruce, who was born John Symon Asher.)

2) Publish a free fan e-mail newsletter

When I give live workshops, I always ask how many attendees have a web site. Usually, about 80 to 90 percent of the hands go up. Great. Then I ask how many publish an e-zine to keep in touch with fans. Only about 25 percent of the hands raise on that one. And that's too bad, because many of those musicians are missing out on one of the most potent online marketing tools.

To illustrate why that is, I need to explain the difference between passive and active marketing. Passive marketing happens when you run an ad, build a web site or pin up fliers. You put your message out there – then you wait and hope that people see your message, understand it and act on it. You can do things to improve its chances of being noticed, but for the most part, you sit on the sidelines, keep your fingers crossed and pray that potential fans will find it and take action.

With active marketing, you don't wait, hope and pray. Instead, you take your message directly to potential fans, one on one. Active marketing includes meeting fans face to face at live shows, sending postcards and other promotional items by snail mail, and sending announcements and updates by e-mail.

To take this more active approach, you must get permission from people to send them more details and special offers. The best places to request that permission are at your live shows and on your web site. No secret here. Bands have been asking people to sign up on mailing lists for years. But you have to take that concept and make it work for you.

That's why, on every page of your web site, you need to make a clear plea for people to sign up on your e-mail list. By signing up, people are in effect saying, "Yeah, I'm interested in what you're doing. Please tell me more."

Once you have their e-mail addresses, you're in control of the conversation. You determine what message they hear, how often they hear it, the tone of the message and so on. There's no sitting back, hoping fans remember you and come back to your site. You actively reach out to these people and repeatedly remind them of all the musical goodies you have waiting for them.

That's why you need to publish a free fan e-mail newsletter. A web site alone is fine. But without an e-mail component to support it, your site is just another billboard passing by on the side of the road.

3) Give it away now

Wouldn't it be great if your name got imbedded into the consciousness of everyone who saw you perform live? Of course. But how can you make that happen? Simply having people in a club while you're playing is a start, but you should strive to make the most of this opportunity and connect with those living, breathing beings in a more meaningful way.

Method: One way to make a stronger connection with fans is to give something free to everyone who attends. Plant a couple of your best, supportive fans at the door and have them pass out some inexpensive item, such as a:

- Small sticker
- Novelty business card with your slogan and web site address on it
- Mailing list sign-up form
- Band newsletter
- Humorous instructions on how to best enjoy your band
- Letterman-like top-10 list

By giving away a freebie, your name and identity sinks in further with fans. Plus, many of these promo items will end up going home with the people who enjoyed you the most – adding more strength to your growing army of fans. And that's not a bad way to go.

4) Take advantage of free entertainment listings

Every city in America has at least one newspaper that covers some aspect of local music and entertainment. And almost all of these publications offer free listings of who's playing where and when – commonly called the "entertainment calendar" section. Believe it or not, live music calendar sections are well read. So why doesn't every band in town take advantage of them?

Perhaps many musicians figure their fans will automatically do all the work necessary to seek them out. Maybe the band members are comfortably lazy with their current level of popularity. Perhaps they think the venue will submit the dates to the papers. (Ha! Guess again.) Maybe they are too busy and simply forget to send in the calendar information.

Key Question: What good does it do to pour your heart and energies into practicing a mind-blowing set and then do nothing to get people out to witness it? Take advantage of every free marketing opportunity available to you; they all contribute to your visibility. So find out when the free listing deadlines are for each paper and then send them your live show schedules regularly!

5) Sponsor an award or special ceremony

Is there a distinguished person in your community you'd like to honor? Or is there an anniversary, special date in history or cause you'd like to recognize? If so, plan a musical event around your chosen theme and make a party out of it.

Under normal circumstances, the local media couldn't care less about your regular weekend gig at Barney's Bar & Grill. But give them a one-time event with a news hook – such as a tribute, awards ceremony, etc. – and you just might have a media landslide on your hands.

6) Sponsor a college or community radio show

Public and community radio stations exist in most major cities these days. Like their PBS television cousins, one of their purposes is to expose segments of the culture that don't get covered in the mainstream media – and that includes local, independent music. These community stations air a wide variety of programs, many of which are sponsored by local businesses. Well, if a local business can sponsor a show, why couldn't an artist or record label?

Sure, it will cost you some money, but it will probably be a lot less than advertising on a commercial station. And you'll be reaching a highly targeted audience – as long as you sponsor a show that attracts the types of people who make up your fan base.

7) Seek out exposure on local cable TV

"The obvious thing you should go for is exposure, and public access TV is your best bet," says Doug Moody, founder of Mystic Records (as quoted in the book *Getting Radio Airplay* by Gary Hustwit). "They have to give you access, they have to expose you. It's amazing how many people actually watch those local access stations."

I hosted a local access music video show in St. Louis, MO, for about four years. It was a low-budget production, but I had a blast doing it. The main benefit was that my image and identity made their way into tens of thousands of households in the area. It's been several years since the show aired, and to this day I occasionally run into someone who asks, "Did you used to host a TV show?" People do watch and remember.

Call the cable TV company that services your area and ask about its lineup of entertainment-related public access shows. With a little persistence, you just might get interviewed or featured in some manner on one of these local programs.

8) Write and record a seasonal or current events-related song

Unless you have friends in high places, your independent CD release barely stands a chance of getting radio airplay on commercial stations. Even the college and community stations require a lot of effort to get a substantial number of spins on the airwaves.

One way to sneak into a station's rotation is to use your creativity and come up with a novelty song that relates to a current topic in the news or an upcoming holiday. For instance, Christmas songs almost always get some airplay during the Yuletide season. But stretch further.

Optional approach: Since you may have a lot of competition during Christmas, try doing songs that pay tribute to more musically obscure holidays – such as Thanksgiving or Groundhog Day. (Come on, how many Groundhog Day songs can you think of?) And what about Easter, Presidents' Day or Columbus Day?

More ideas: What about songs pertaining to a local political scandal, sports team or election? How about putting a local slant on Halloween, the Fourth of July or Valentine's Day? Or have you considered recording a jingle or theme song for one of the popular morning radio shows? Use your imagination! Anything's possible with this marketing angle.

Believe it or not, novelty songs have a much better chance of getting commercial airplay – which will get your name out there, possibly paving the way for your more serious songs later. Just make sure the novelty or theme song you write and pitch to the station is in line with your overall musical style and identity.

9) Multiply your press exposure

When you get a review or feature story published in the press, make copies of it and send it to everyone on your industry contact list – including radio stations, record stores, music publications, nightclub owners and booking agents. Reinforce your recognition factor with the people who are most likely to help you get even more exposure. And don't forget to include press clippings (or at least excerpted quotes from them) in mailings that go to your fans.

10) Target specific cities and regions for best results

You don't need to do live shows across the country, coast to coast, to effectively promote your music. In fact, it will probably be better for your exposure level and record sales (not to mention your sanity) to zero in on a predetermined number of cities.

Example: "You shouldn't spread yourself too thin," says Rob Squires, bassist for the Denver, CO-based Big Head Todd & the Monsters. Before landing its record deal, the band took this approach: "To establish ourselves, we'd hit Chicago, San Francisco, Austin and the Colorado cities every other month," Squires told *Fast Forward*, a newsletter put out by Disc Makers.

Result: "Our plan worked out great. There'd be more and more people at shows each time we revisited those target cities." By focusing on a limited number of geographic areas, Big Head Todd & the Monsters was able to build a following and was later signed to a record label that could give them nationwide support.

11) Ask nightclub owners to play your songs in their radio and TV commercials

Surely, of all the venues at which you perform, at least some of them advertise on the radio and television. And practically all of those commercials use music underneath the announcer's voice or video, right? Why not encourage the club owner to use one of your original songs for that purpose?

Lesson: It's the next best thing to being put into regular rotation on a radio station, even though you'll only be able to squeeze a verse and chorus, at most, into a commercial. But just think, you won't have to pull teeth with a program director and compete with hundreds of other new releases to get your music on the air. All you have to do is be persuasive with the club owner and get to him or her with this idea before the other band's that play the club.

Warning: You might have to negotiate with the owner to get this special treatment – remember, he or she is footing the bill for the paid ad spot. Some things to offer might include performing at the club for a reduced fee or offering part of your pay to help cover some of the ad costs. Either way, it might be worth it to get even a minute of your original music on commercial radio or local TV.

12) Offer an inexpensive CD sampler of your music

If you've ever visited a Sam's Club or a large grocery store on a busy weekend, you've no doubt encountered lots of opportunities to sample free food. Whether they're new, improved pizza rolls or a new brand of zesty sausage, food companies love getting free samples into the mouths of potential buyers.

In the same way, you should be whetting the appetites of music fans with free and low-cost samples of your music ... then reeling them in to purchase your full-length recordings.

How to Do It: Pick two or three songs off of your current or upcoming release. Or, if you have a few releases out, create a short "best of" compilation. Then produce a couple hundred of these sampler CDs – whether you burn them yourself or go through a replication company.

Don't worry too much about frills at this stage. Pour all your artistic detail into the final full-length product. Keep these samplers simple and low-cost, so you can give away and sell a lot of them without losing your shirt.

Some bands successfully sell sampler tapes for one or two dollars to cover costs. Fans who are willing to part with a buck or two will probably be more willing to spend $10 to $15 on your full CD. If you do give away samplers, you should consider requiring fans to sign up on your mailing list before they get the freebie.

Important Tip: While the CD sampler artwork should be inexpensive, one thing you absolutely must print on it is your web site address and specific instructions on how to order your full-length releases. That's the whole point of these music samplers: To increase your notoriety, your mailing list and the sales of your recorded products.

13) Ask your fans to help you get gigs and airplay

A wise person once said, "You won't get things in life unless you ask for them." Use that same philosophy when it comes to your fans. Don't be shy about asking the people who like your music the most to be a part of your success story. There are two key ways to accomplish this:

- In all of your mailings to your fans, include the names and phone numbers of radio stations you are targeting for airplay. Then encourage your fans to call these stations and request that your music be played. You can also distribute fliers at your live shows that offer this same radio contact information.

- While you're asking your fans for help with airplay, why not ask for their help in getting paid band jobs? You never know who among your fans knows a club owner or someone having a private function with a budget for live entertainment. You might even entice your fans further by offering a 10 percent commission on whatever you make through the job they help you book. Why not? That's free enterprise at its best!

Take these 13 promotional ideas and make them work for you.

Chapter 13

20 Things You Should Be Doing Right Now to Promote Your Music Better

There are literally thousands of strategies that successful songwriters, bands and record labels have used over the years to promote themselves more effectively. What follows are 20 techniques and ideas you can start using today to spread the word about your music. There are three key words in that last sentence. Two are *start using*; the third is *today*! Take those words to heart as you absorb these ideas and motivate yourself to put them into action.

At the very least, I implore you to choose one tactic out of these 20 and get moving on it. Starting today!

1) Write a letter to the editor

Respond to a music-related topic in your local newspaper or a national magazine. Work in a mention of your band. As long as you have an insightful comment and are subtle about plugging yourself, chances are good it will end up in print.

2) Use a strong headline in ads, fliers, posters and web pages

Album cover graphics and other artwork are great, but research shows that bold, attention-getting headlines (with more details following in the smaller-size body copy) pull the most response.

3) Include complete contact info on every promotional item you send

Bios and press releases get separated from CDs and photos. Don't leave anything to chance. Include your name, address, phone, fax, e-mail and web site address on every piece of marketing communication you send out or give away.

4) Commit to connecting with one music fan at a time

Unlike the major labels, you don't have to market to millions of people and sell 200,000 copies of your CD to be successful. Commit to working at the grassroots level, connecting with one new fan at a time. At first, you'll have 10 followers. Then 100, then 500, and eventually 1,000 and more. Take the personal approach of slowly but surely building up your notoriety.

5) Use testimonials and positive review quotes

Don't just use your press clippings and fan mail to impress mom and dad. Positive quotes from third-party sources add lots of clout toward your efforts to get press, airplay, gigs and more. And don't just wait for them to come to you. Ask radio, newspaper, nightclub and other industry people you know for a line you can use in your media kit. Make this an ongoing activity.

6) Ask politely but firmly for action

Whether your goal is to get a CD review, radio airplay or a paid gig, always make sure to *ask* for what you want. Don't apologize. Don't beat around the bush. Don't wimp out. Just ask! And do it pleasantly and confidently.

7) Provide take-one boxes to record stores and nightclubs

Keep your eye out for small cardboard boxes you can recycle into "take one" containers. Print small handout fliers that promote the availability of your new release or dates of your upcoming shows. Place these in the boxes, which should be covered with artwork and text that says: "Hey You! Take one of these." Then ask local record store and nightclub managers if you can place these unique boxes in their establishments. Chances are, you'll be the only artist in town doing this.

8) Offer a tongue-in-cheek report or survey

Take a poll of your fans, interview people on the streets or just act as if you have ... it doesn't matter. This may not be scientific research, but it is a fun way to hook the media into covering you.

Let's say you came up with the results of a survey titled "The Top Ten Reasons Local Music Fans Hate the Jerry Spinger Show" or "The Startling Reality of What Toledo Nightclub-Goers Think of Madonna as a Mother." If it's funny and timely enough, a lot of the newspapers, magazines and Internet sources you contact will mention your survey. Some may even run all of your survey results – while plugging the source: you. Also include this survey in a newsletter to your fans.

9) Have an attitude/take a stand

Musicians who try to be all things to all people usually come up short when promoting themselves. The most successful artists know who they are, know what they stand for and aren't afraid of alienating many segments of the population when expressing themselves. Sure, you may rub some music fans the wrong way. But the fans who do identify with you will back you all the way.

10) Present a music-related contest

In the same way that surveys and tongue-in-cheek reports (listed earlier) can lead to public awareness, so can contests bring you valuable exposure. They can either be serious (a Guitar Player Challenge, your basic Battle of the Bands) or more light-hearted (Stupid Musician Tricks, the World's Largest Twister Game).

One guy in my hometown presents an annual Night of a Thousand Spoons, during which hordes of musicians play ... you guessed it, spoons. And it gets press every year. The best contests, though, will tie in nicely with your band name, album title or overall musical identity. Find one that works for you.

11) Supply your fans with a list of radio station phone numbers

There's a good chance you already ask your fans to call radio stations and request your music. It can help create a groundswell of support. But do you also supply the radio station phone numbers? That's the key: Don't make your fans do extra work to look up numbers. In all of your fan communications, list station call letters *and* their phone numbers ... and then beg your supporters to make those calls!

12) Get on other bands' mailing lists

Countless songwriters and bands are doing all kinds of things to promote themselves. Most of them use ho-hum methods. But every now and then you run across a real promotional gem. Wouldn't you like to be aware of those gems more often? Sign up on the mailing lists of many other artists. Start observing how these groups and record labels promote themselves. "Borrow" some of the better ideas and discard the rest.

13) Develop a music business and personal development library

I'm beginning to hate the phrase "Knowledge is power." Not only is it overused, but the truth is, knowledge without taking the steps to use it creatively and effectively is useless. That said, I still encourage you to absorb as much info as you can on the music business. The best way to do that is to build a music business library.

The bookcases in my home resemble the how-to and self-help sections of a Barnes & Noble. My shelves are stocked not only with music industry-related titles, they're also filled with volumes on publicity, small business marketing, time management, sales techniques, positive thinking, nutrition, spirituality and much more. My personal library serves as a constant reminder of the areas I need to stay sharp on, and I quite frequently pull out a book for a quick refresher course on whatever topic I need help with. You'd be wise to do the same thing.

14) Follow up on everything

This should be a no-brainer, but you'd be surprised by the number of people who pay lip service to the concept of follow-through and still end up overlooking it. The idea here is simple: If you tell someone you're going to send a package, for example … make sure you do it! Once the package is sent, follow up with a phone call or e-mail to make sure the person received it. Wait a couple of weeks (or however long is appropriate for the situation) and call again to get the status of the review, feature story, gig or whatever it is you're after.

Don't expect other people or the whims of fate to take care of your career. Grab the reins and stay on top of your promotional activities. Doing so will virtually guarantee that good things will come your way.

15) Get the Correct Spelling of People's Names

If you've heard me share this story before, here it is again: I've grown tired of getting mail and phone calls directed to Bob Barker. My last name is Baker. It always has been and always will be (unless I feel the need to change my identity like Prince did). I am not a game show host. And if I were, I'd much prefer something like *Love Connection* over *The Price Is Right*.

The point: Anyone who refers to me as Bob Barker starts off with a serious mark against them. It tells me they haven't done their homework and are probably rushing through the motions of promoting themselves. So my advice to you is slow down and make sure you:

- Have the name of a specific person to contact
- Are certain he or she is the proper person you need to be contacting
- Get the exact spelling of the person's name

16) Send thank-you notes

This is a simple act, but it really does make a difference. When a writer does a story on your band or when a disc jockey plays one of your songs during her show, send a quick note of thanks. These small acts of random kindness do make an impression on the people receiving them. And it just may cause your industry connections to have a cozier attitude toward you the next time you approach them for a favor. Buy a box of 20 or so inexpensive thank-you cards and have them handy whenever someone does something to help you. Or have a template set up on your computer and personalize each card as you print it.

17) Communicate with people (at times) when you don't want anything from them

Success in the music business has as much to do with the quality of your relationships as it does the quality of your music. One of your goals should be to make friends and fans of people who are in a real position to help further your career.

But a friendship is a two-way transaction. If you only communicate with someone when you need something from him or her, the relationship is not on a balanced, solid ground. That's why you should get in the habit of calling, mailing, faxing and e-mailing your music industry contacts occasionally when you want nothing from them at all. Call and ask how a recent holiday went, to wish them a happy birthday, to pass along some information you came across that might interest them, etc.

You should always have a specific objective in mind any time you communicate with someone, but your objective doesn't always have to be self-serving.

18) Be able to describe your music and image in 10 words or less

When you finally get a music editor or program director on the phone, he might very well ask, "So what kind of music do you play?" How will you respond? By hem-hawing around about how unique your sound is and how you "hate labels"? Don't get caught in this trap.

You should be able to define your music and image in 10 words or less." There are two primary reasons:

1) So you can quickly communicate your sound and identity to media sources, industry people and potential fans alike

2) So you can use it as a gauge by which to focus all of your songs, titles, artwork, photos, ads and more around a consistent theme

People (including you) shouldn't be confused about what they get from you and your music.

For more details on this topic, read about Brand Identity Statements in Chapter 2.

19) Supply a list of questions for radio and TV interviewers

When you get invited to do a radio or TV interview – whether it's for the local college radio station, public access TV or VH1 – you're being handed a great chance to get your message out to the public and connect with thousands of new fans. Don't blow the opportunity by sending a watered-down, ambiguous message.

Interviewers might have good intentions, but if they're not given a road map, there's no telling what tangent they might veer off on while speaking to you on the air. That's why supplying them with a list of questions and topics can help keep your message on track.

Of course, even when you do offer suggested questions, the interviewer may ignore them. When this happens, find a sensible, non-threatening way to steer the conversation back to the specific ideas you want to get across regarding who you are and what you play.

20) Write down a plan of action

While you want to be flexible enough to take advantage of promotional opportunities that spring up unexpectedly, nothing beats having a solid plan of action. And writing down your plans gives it substance. To help craft the best plan, ask yourself the following questions:

- What specific message do I want to get across to music fans and industry people?
- What are the best methods to get that idea across?
- What creative tactics should I pursue first in my effort to promote myself?
- What should I do next?

Write down your answers to these questions and develop a more refined plan. Then take the first step and get busy. The plan is always subject to change, but simply having one in the first place gets you moving toward your goals. Action, energy and movement lead to new opportunities, open doors and unexpected good fortune.

For more on effective planning and goal setting, turn back to Chapter 1.

As I mentioned at the beginning of this chapter, pick at least one of these 20 promotional ideas and start working on it today!

Guerrilla Music Marketing
Activity Worksheets – #2

What are your top 5 skills (musical and otherwise)?

1. _____
2. _____
3. _____
4. _____
5. _____

How are you currently selling your CDs, tapes and other merchandise?

_____
_____
_____
_____
_____

What steps could you take to increase sales through these current channels?

_____
_____
_____
_____
_____

What other sales avenues should you be pursuing but aren't yet?

_____
_____
_____
_____
_____
_____

What new strategies could you use to sell more music through ...

Retail stores:

_____

_____

_____

Distributors:

_____

_____

_____

Live shows:

_____

_____

_____

Direct mail:

_____

_____

_____

The Internet:

_____

_____

_____

Mail order catalogs:

_____

_____

_____

Other creative methods:

_____

_____

_____

What negative beliefs do you have about your potential to succeed with your music?

_____

_____

_____

_____

What positive, empowering beliefs do you have about your potential to succeed with your music?

_____

_____

_____

_____

How might you develop a more enthusiastic outlook on your journey toward success?

_____

_____

_____

_____

Make a list of encouraging things that have happened to you in the past year or so:

_____

_____

_____

_____

List some ways you can "give more than you get" from your music business contacts:

_____

_____

_____

_____

List some ways you might raise extra money for your Guerrilla Music Project Fund:

_____

_____

_____

_____

_____

What people/sources might you turn to for a loan?

_____

_____

_____

_____

What skills/possessions/resources might you offer someone in a barter situation?

_____

_____

_____

_____

What other creative tactics could you use to get the recording time, equipment or production services you need?

_____

_____

_____

_____

Make a list of obvious, traditional methods of getting exposure for your music:

_____

_____

_____

_____

Now brainstorm on offbeat, overlooked, even crazy ideas on how to ...

Get more (and better) gigs:

_____

_____

_____

Get exposure in the print media:

_____

_____

_____

Get radio airplay:

_____

_____

_____

Get exposure on the Internet:

_____

_____

_____

Attract new fans:

_____

_____

_____

Get exposure on television:

_____

_____

Earn extra money:

_____

_____

_____

Other thoughts and ideas to turbo-charge your career:

_____

_____

_____

Bonus Special Reports Section

Killer Press Kits: The 29 Most Important Elements in Creating Sizzling Music Publicity Materials – page 116

How to Double Your CD Sales (in 90 Days or Less) – page 125

High-Impact Promotional Strategies You Should Be Using to Market Your Music – page 131

The Easiest Way to Make Money in the Music Business: Create Multiple Streams of Income – page 140

7 Crucial Music Marketing Steps You Need to Be Taking Right Now – page 145

25 Tips to Help You Market Your Music Through the Mail – page 150

Advertising Your Music: How to Make It Pay (and Avoid the Most Common Mistakes) – page 156

Killer Press Kits: The 29 Most Important Elements in Creating Sizzling Music Publicity Materials

Sometimes it's called a press kit. Other times it's referred to as a promo package or media kit. Whatever you call it, this collection of music marketing tools will help you get more gigs, media exposure, radio airplay, industry attention and more.

However, I should also remind you that over 95 percent of the press kits sent out by bands and record labels end up in the trashcan. Those aren't very good odds. It's not easy to get pumped up when you consider that rate of failure.

But there's a good reason all those press kits are being ignored: Most of the promo packages clogging up the postal system are lackluster attempts at marketing. They are hastily thrown together without much thought or purpose behind them.

I know this with certainty because for 10 years I published a music magazine in the Midwest. I've seen enough bad media kits to make anyone's head spin. But I also recall the rare gems that caught my attention – the well-thought-out press kits that sold me on an act's worthiness, inspired me to pop in a CD and quickly motivated me to assign a feature story on the act.

To make sure a lot more of your press kits are actually read and acted upon, please consider the following tips – what I consider to be the 29 most important elements of a successful promo package.

Soak up this advice and put it to use right away!

Cover Letter

Any time you send a press kit, it should be accompanied with a cover letter written to a human being at the publication, radio station, booking agency, record label, etc. This first element of your kit serves the all-important purpose of intriguing the recipient and spelling out the reasons he or she should bother looking through the rest of the kit.

Here are the main points to keep in mind when crafting this introductory letter:

Address the letter to a specific person

"Dear editor" won't cut it. Call and find out the exact name of the person who handles the area in which you want to make an impact. And get the correct spelling of that person's name!

It should be the first thing the person sees

Place the cover letter on top. If the rest of the items in your press kit are neatly presented in a folder (which is a good idea), the cover letter should be paper-clipped to the outside of the front cover.

The cover letter should be no longer than one page

Make your letter relatively short and sweet. Lengthy, rambling cover letters get set aside (or thrown away). Make your pitch quickly ... and then get out of the way. After all, it's the other items in the kit that you want the person to really spend time reading.

It should speak directly to the person receiving it

Don't use your cover letter to brag about yourself. Instead, use it to show the recipient that you understand his or her position and the problems he or she faces. Then briefly describe why your musical story provides a solution and helps meet his or her needs.

Of course, if you've already communicated with the person before, point that out in the letter. If he or she has requested your material, make that very clear. If it's a cold submission, state your best case quickly and interestingly.

Write in a conversational tone

If I read one more "Per our telephone conversation ..." I'm going to strangle someone. Commit this tip to memory: Write like you talk. If you wouldn't say it that way to someone face to face, don't phrase it that way in a cover letter.

Let me clarify: Write like you talk as long as you don't talk like an idiot. You must write your cover letter intelligently. Just don't try to sound overly professional to the point that you sound pompous. People in the music business want to connect with other humans, not survey a document that reads like a college term paper.

Start with a sensible grabber

It helps when the opening sentence of your cover letter grabs the reader's attention.

Examples:

"Hi, my name is Fred and I manage a band called..." – BAD

"I'm sure most of the 800 people at our recent CD release party are readers of your fine paper." – BETTER (but it reeks of butt-kissing)

"When was the last time you heard a banjo player in a heavy metal band?" – BEST (this opening sentence is truly newsworthy, as long as there really is a banjo player in your heavy metal band)

End with a P.S.

You should always have one or two major points, at most, to make in your cover letter. Take the most important point and repeat it in a P.S. along with a tempting call to action.

Example: "P.S. I know your readers appreciate being exposed to new trends in music. Heavy metal banjo players aren't exactly a dime a dozen. Please call me at the number above for more details. I'll even send you a free T-shirt!"

News Release

A news release is a sheet that spells out the nitty-gritty on a specific event or newsworthy topic. Typical subjects include a new CD release, a special upcoming show, a personal appearance at a record store. News releases can also alert the media about upcoming TV show appearances, when a band reaches a noteworthy radio or sales chart status, info on a departing or new band member, etc.

Here are some tips to keep in mind when writing a news release:

Make it no longer than one page

Again, brevity is king. Lay out the important facts swiftly and simply. Don't make your readers wade through paragraph after paragraph of useless verbiage.

Limit the scope to one angle

A good news release doesn't tell your life story. It covers only one sliver of your activities. Don't write a release about your new CD *and* the band's new singer *and* the charity show next month. Craft a separate news release for each topic.

Put the meaty details up front

The traditional advice on news releases says to include the who, what, where, when and why in the first paragraph. If you can do that in an interesting way, go for it.

I'm not such a stickler for that wisdom, but do get to the point early and make sure all basic questions about your topic are answered somewhere in the news release.

Artist Bio

As you should know, "bio" is short for "biography." An effective artist bio gives more detailed background information on the act and spells out the current state of things with your music.

A bio should be no longer than two pages

While an artist bio can take up more room to tell your story, don't think of it as an encyclopedia. I've seen many bios that run a few pages, but these usually contain more facts than a media person needs to know. One or two pages at the most is plenty of space to share your musical life. Here are the five elements of a good artist bio:

The best band bios read like magazine articles

Like many of the editors you'll be contacting, I enjoy reading bios that have the feel of a feature story in a newspaper or magazine. I don't want a list of facts and accomplishments. But I do like to discover those things as I read an interesting tale about your music.

Use quotes from key people

A good feature story-type of bio will intersperse exposition with quotes from the main player (or players) in your act. If there is another party involved in your story (such as a nightclub, charity or record store), get quotes from a person at that establishment too. Weaving in positive quotes from published reviews is also acceptable within a bio.

Be positive, but don't over-hype

Your bio should definitely put an optimistic spin on your musical activities. However, crossing the line and being too boastful can work against you. Writing that your band "has been causing a stir in Chicago with energetic live shows" is cool. Saying you're "the hottest thing since the Beatles and Elvis" is downright silly.

Write your bio as if a publication might run the entire thing

There's another reason to go easy on the hype. Many small publications may run some or all of your bio as an article. Most people who run music publications are overworked and underpaid. And there is always a shortage of well-written material to run. Give them something that's cleanly worded and interesting, and they just might run it as is.

Recorded Music

Your goal with media people is similar to your goal with fans. You want to motivate them to take the time to listen to your music. Listening to – and then enjoying – your songs is what turns casual listeners into diehard fans and indifferent editors into media cheerleaders for your music. Follow the suggestions in this section to improve your chances of getting your music heard by the media.

CDs vs. cassettes vs. DVDs

This is another one of those things that should go without saying, but just in case you're still living in the Dark Ages ... After having received many thousands of packages over the years, I can tell you that CDs are clearly the format of choice. And for all the obvious reasons: sound quality, convenience and the ease of cueing up individual tracks.

Some time, just for fun, pop in a cassette you're not familiar with and try finding the beginning of the second song ... then the third song. It's frustrating and time consuming. So you can imagine how thrilled overworked media people are when they have to awkwardly skip through a tape to get a feel for a new release.

Note: If you think everyone receiving your press kit is going to play your recording all the way through, guess again. Most of them will breeze through it to determine if your album is worth a more in-depth listening. CDs make this process infinitely easier. And that's your job – to make it as easy as possible for people to give you press, radio airplay, paid gigs and more.

If you have a music DVD of your act available, I offer you the same warning I used to give regarding VHS videos. It's hard enough to get media people to spend a couple of minutes listening to your audio-only CD. Expecting they'll drop everything to turn on a TV or watch your DVD on a computer is risky. So proceed with caution.

If you want to reach a lot of media sources and simply can't afford to send everyone a CD, do this: Send CDs to your high-priority contacts and places most likely to respond. Send your low-priority contacts a news release, bio and photo. In a cover letter that goes with them, ask the recipient to contact you if they want a free review copy. That way, you send CDs only to the people who really want them.

Take off the shrink-wrap

It may seem like a minor thing, but it does take some effort to pry off that impenetrable plastic that surrounds new CDs, cassettes and DVDs. Imagine being pressed for time and having to wrestle with a dozen (or more) of these babies at one sitting. Again, make it easy for people to enjoy your music and you will be rewarded!

Make sure contact info is on the CD/cassette itself *and* the case it came in

I'll admit it, I'm a contact information freak. If you're going to be a lean, mean, self-promotion machine, you must do everything you can to get people (both industry folks and fans) to connect with you. Sending out your press kit and then expecting people to jump through hoops to figure out how to get in touch with you is pure madness.

Cover letters get separated from bios. Photos get removed from related news releases. CD sleeves drift away from the discs they identify. Put your contact info on everything! Think of your music marketing tools as frisky puppies that love to break from the leash and run away. They need identification tags so the people who find them know who they belong to.

Photo

Another one of your goals is to help media people put a face to your name and sound. A good artist photo will do that. But good photos are rare. When you do have an intriguing, professional-looking photo, media people remember you – and your photo ends up in print and online more often. Here are some artist photo tips to consider:

Close-ups are better than wide shots

The best photos, generally speaking, are up close and personal. A tight shot on the members' faces is far more appealing than a wide-angle view of a band running through a field. And if you're a solo artist, you should definitely use photos with a close-up view. Keep the shapes and images in your photos simple and large – let them fill up the frame.

Keep backgrounds simple

The emphasis in your photo should be on the artist. But you'd be shocked by the number of pictures I've seen that feature musicians posing in front of busy, mind-numbing background scenes. After all, it is called an *artist* photo, not a background photo. Picking a location that has atmosphere and texture is cool, as long as you make sure that you and your band members stand out against it.

Avoid straight lines and dull arrangements

If your photographer asks you and your band mates to stand in an orderly, straight line while he or she shoots at eye level, run the other way. Don't do this, unless you plan on giving out smelling salts with all your photos.

Better approaches: Stagger the positions of the players. Try sitting or laying down. Have the photographer shoot from a high angle above or low angle below.

Or play with special effects lenses (as long as the visual effects don't blur the people in the picture too much).

Dress and pose members so they look like they're all in the same band

Did you ever see the "We Are the World" charity video from the 1980s? You had rockers and R&B players standing next to pop stars and folk singers. That's great for a cooperative charity event, but it's plain lousy for your band photo. Unfortunately, way too many band photos have this disjointed, mix-and-match feel.

Long before the photo shoot, every member should have a handle on what identity the band needs to portray. Dress accordingly. The attitudes and facial expressions also need to gel. One guy can't be scowling while another sports a goofy grin. Bottom line: Have a consistent look and attitude.

Supply digital images in both high- and low-resolution formats

Your photos can be used in many ways. But there are two ways you need to be most concerned with: in print and on the Web. So, in addition to sending a nice hard copy black-and-white or color photo with your press kit, it will also help to let the media know that you have digital images available in high- and low-resolution formats.

For use on web sites, low-resolution images are needed (usually JPEG files saved at 72 pixels per inch). For reproduction in print, most publications will want a high-resolution image (often saved as a TIF file at 150 to 300 dots per inch).

Whether your photos are shot using a digital camera to begin with or they are prints that you scan, find a way to convert your photos to these digital formats. And, to make it easy for media people to access them, make them available for download from a special media section of your web site.

Photos versus lithographs

Photographs are the nice, slick pictures that magazines prefer getting. The 8" x 10" size is still the industry standard, although good 5" x 7" prints work well, too. Lithographs are half-toned images of your photograph reproduced using offset printing. They look pretty good and are a lot less expensive, but beware: Lithographs don't reproduce as well as real photos in publications. Many magazines and newspapers won't use them.

Best advice: Use high-quality photos to send to the media. Get the more affordable lithographs to give away to fans and pin up at nightclubs, etc.

Press Clippings

It's a funny thing. Media exposure often leads to more media exposure. Therefore, you want editors and writers to see what other media have already written about you. Plus, you want radio people and nightclub owners to know what kind of exposure you're getting. The best way to let them know about the growing buzz over your music is through a collection of press clippings. Here are three things to keep in mind when compiling your press clippings:

Use photocopies

Don't make the mistake of sending pages (sometimes called "tear sheets") from the original publications that your write-ups appeared in. Instead, make attractive photocopies of those write-ups. For one thing, it can be difficult and expensive to get enough of the original publications to send to everyone on your media list. Most importantly, editors won't be any more impressed by the original than they will by a copy.

Also, basic black and white copies will do just fine. There's no need to print your press clippings in color, unless you have one or two pages that are particularly striking – and you can justify the extra cost to send color copies to prime media contacts.

Arrange your clippings neatly on each page

Every time you get reviewed or featured in the press, take the issue and cut out the section in which your piece appears. If it fits on a standard 8.5" x 11" sheet, great. If not, find a print shop with a good photocopier and reduce or enlarge the section to fit nicely on a page.

It's also a good idea to take the flag (the publication's logo and name from the front cover) and place it on the same page along with the date of the issue. This obviously lets people know the origin of each write-up. And when you have a few shorter blurbs on your band that aren't substantial enough for their own page, combine them all on one sheet. Just make sure they are all properly labeled by publication and date.

Staple your press clipping sheets together

While you want to keep your bio, press release and cover letter as loose sheets, all of your press clippings should be stapled together. Especially if you have a lot of clippings, this makes it easier for the recipient to flip through them without having to juggle reams of loose paper.

Positive Quotes Page

As we already discussed, a media person will rarely listen to your CD all the way through – especially the first time. The same goes for reading all of the articles and reviews included in your press clippings. That's where the Positive Quotes Page comes into play. Use these two tips to create yours:

Weed out highlights from published reviews

You know that sprinkled throughout all of the write-ups you've earned are some golden nuggets of praise. I suggest you do what major motion picture marketers do: Pull out the best one- or two-sentence quotes from a variety of media sources, as in "'Two thumbs up!' –Roger Ebert." Go through all of the published write-ups in your collection of press clippings and find the most sparkling endorsements.

Examples: "Acme Rock Band sizzles on its debut CD!" –*The Podunk Gazette*

"The new disc from Acme Rock Band is chock full of catchy, three-minute pop gems." –*New Music Dispatch*

Take these quotes and print them in large type on a single page. You might put a headline at the top that reads: "Here's what the media is saying about Acme Rock Band ..." I'd even suggest using this positive quotes sheet as the cover page for your stapled collection of press clippings. That way, someone could get a quick overview of the great things media sources have been saying about you. And the full-length articles are in the same package for those who want to read a little deeper.

Ask select industry people for a comment to include in your kit

What if you're just starting out or have a newly formed band? You may not have any (or many) positive quotes or press clippings. Now what?

Approach people you know in the music business (nightclub owners, studio engineers, disc jockeys) and ask them for a comment you can use. "I can always count on The Porcupines to put on a great show at my club!" –Ted Smith, owner, the Cool Club. That's a good start when you're short on traditional media quotes.

Also, when gathering these blurbs, feel free to suggest the wording for the person's comment. He or she can always change or tweak it, but you may be surprised by how many people will accept the blurb you wrote as is and let you use it on your Positive Quotes Page.

Now you have the recipe (29 ingredients, to be exact) for cooking up a sizzling press kit. It's time to get busy and promote yourself!

How to Double Your CD Sales (in 90 Days or Less)

If you've gone through the trouble of recording and manufacturing a CD release, you no doubt want to sell some of them. Preferably, a lot of them. Here are a couple dozen ways to make that happen in the next 90 days or less:

Write great songs and create meaningful music

While the purpose of this report does not include songwriting advice, it should be noted that all the marketing help in the world won't be effective unless the music you make profoundly touches people. Writing great music needs to be one of your driving forces. So make sure you spend enough time on this crucial area.

Put a priority on planning and execution

Think of these twin soldiers as your offensive line. Planning (knowing where you want to go and what route you're going to take) and execution (marching toward your goal by taking decisive action) are the ingredients you'll need to double your CD sales. Set weekly and monthly sales goals, and monitor your progress regularly to make sure you're on track.

Bring back past customers

It costs about six times more money and effort to win over a new fan than it does to stay in touch with someone who bought a previous CD or has been to one of your shows. Don't overlook this gold mine. Send special offers to people who have spent money on you in the past. They are, by far, the most likely group of music people to spend money on you.

Upsell current customers

Okay, so someone comes to a gig, buys your latest CD and signs up on your mailing list. Now what? Time to move on to the next new customer, right? Wrong. Send your current buyers a special offer to also get your previous releases.

Your first or second CD may be old news to you, but it will probably be fresh and enjoyable to a new fan. He or she likes your music and even bought your new CD.

Don't deny them the pleasure of getting even more of your music – both old and new. Strike while the music sales iron is hot. It's called "upselling," and you'll have to start doing it if you really want to double your CD sales.

Always be cultivating new customers

Marketing music is a juggling act. You have to simultaneously be courting past fans and nudging current buyers while always being on the lookout for new fans to bring into the fold. You cultivate these new people by:

- Encouraging mailing list sign-ups at gigs
- Talking to the people who attend your live shows
- Constantly soliciting fan e-mail newsletter subscriptions online
- Giving solid reasons for editors, writers and reviewers to cover you
- Swapping web site links and e-mail newsletter line ads with other related web sites and e-zines
- Putting your contact info on every promotional item you distribute
- Generally making it easy for people to find you and get in touch

In short, make a commitment to being a fan-building machine.

Identify your most profitable selling areas

In order to double your CD sales in 90 days, you must know where and how to concentrate your energies. First, consider if geography will play a part. Will you most likely sell more CDs locally? In the Midwest? Along the East Coast? In Denmark? Next, consider the method of sales: Mail order, retail sales, distributors, sales at gigs, the Internet ... which ones will work best for you?

Understand who your ideal fans are

Determine what type of person is most likely to spend money on you: young or old, men or women, lavish tastes or budget-minded, hyper or mellow? Other questions to ask: Do these people have the money to buy your CDs? And is this segment of the population growing in number or shrinking? Are there any other ways of positioning your music to also appeal to a different group of people? Write answers to these questions, brainstorm and zero in on fans who will buy your music.

List ways of getting access to your fans

Once you know exactly what type of music fan you're going after, make a list of various ways to communicate with these specific people. What magazines and newspapers do they read? Where do they hang out? What radio stations do they listen to? What retail outlets do they frequent? What web sites do they surf to? What e-mail newsletters do they subscribe to?

List every conceivable way of reaching these important folks. Then design an action plan to make the most of these avenues.

Tour and play live often

Sure, this is a no-brainer, but are you making the most of every possibility? First, are you playing out a lot locally and regionally? Does your touring plan make sense? The best approach is to either spiral out slowly but surely from your home base, or target specific cities you will play on a regular schedule. The more areas you're known in, the better your chances of selling more CDs.

And what about unplugged shows at record stores, coffeehouses and more offbeat locations like bookstores and art galleries? Refer back to the list of places where your fans hang out and try to perform at those venues.

Make the most of retail store tie-ins

Have you visited all the important music shops and arranged to have your CDs sold there? If so, do managers have sample copies for in-store play? If the store has a listening station, can you get your disc featured on it? Will the store use discount coupons for your release as a bag stuffer (maybe in exchange for you distributing coupons for the store at your gigs)? Be creative and sell more CDs!

Pursue radio exposure of any kind

Of course, you can mail unsolicited CDs and hound program directors until either they play your songs or you give up trying. Or you can use some often-overlooked tactics to get on the air: Supply stations with several of your CDs to give away as part of an on-air promotion. Write and record a humorous theme song for high-profile shows and on-air personalities.

Find a current event tie-in to one of your songs and get interviewed on the air about it. Ask nightclub owners who advertise to use your songs in the bed of their radio (and TV) commercials. Buy cheap overnight ads to promote your new release.

Use sensible, low-cost advertising

Put together a short, inexpensive sampler CD of your songs (or a group of bands' songs) and offer them for a buck or two through classified line ads in regional and national music publications. You'll be lucky to break even on this with up-front sales, but if you follow up and persuade even 5 to 10 percent of these folks to buy your full-length CD, it could be well worth it.

Squeeze all you can out of the Internet

The Web has most definitely become the great equalizer. It's easier than ever for independent artists to reach a worldwide audience. A big chunk of web activity is dedicated to music, and it seems there are more sites every month that sell indie CDs or cater in some way to unsigned acts and small record labels. You need to be using the Internet to spread the word about your music. Thousands of artists are already doing it. Now go get your share!

Here are some steps you can take to sell more CDs online:

Get your own domain name

While there are many music web sites that will offer you a free page or section, your best bet is to register your own domain name and direct it to wherever you choose to host your pages. There are two big benefits: A web address like www.johnsmithmusic.com carries more credibility and is easier to remember than a long and winding address like www.musichotspot.com/music/johnsmith. Plus, most major search engines these days are not listing the free hosting URLs because they generally don't last long. Registered domains are simply taken more seriously. And rates have never been cheaper.

One of the most popular sites for registering low-cost domain names is **Go Daddy** at www.godaddy.com. Fees are only $8.95 per year. **DirectNIC** at www.directnic.com is another good one, with domain name fees of $15 a year.

Publish a fan e-mail newsletter

Web sites are great, but they're basically online billboards seen by surfers passing in the night. To sell more CDs, you absolutely must collect the e-mail addresses of people who have willingly agreed to get regular follow-up messages on your musical activities.

Therefore, you have to start promoting your free music newsletter like it's the coolest thing since Napster. Offer people incentives to sign up. Having a large and growing subscriber list is one of your biggest keys to online sales and notoriety. To help you manage your list, there are services that can help. Here are three:

Ezine Director
www.ezinedirector.com

Topica
www.topica.com

Yahoo! Groups
http://groups.yahoo.com/

Make sure your fans can order securely online

If you make sales only to people who snail mail checks and money orders, your CD sales progress will remain slow and painful. The good news is that there are a seemingly infinite number of options for accepting credit cards online.

CD Baby, www.cdbaby.com – A one-time $35 fee gets you completely set up with audio samples, CD artwork, band bio and more. CD Baby is the premier site for indie music sales and is very credible and reliable.

Amazon.com Advantage Program – www.amazon.com/exec/obidos/subst/partners/direct/advantage-for-music.html – If you have a UPC code imprinted on your CD, you'll be able to get listed on the planet's largest, most active e-commerce site. Sign up for Amazon's Advantage program and get access to millions of music buyers.

Pay Pal, www.PayPal.com, is yet another service that allows you to accept online payments ... with no up-front costs. Fees are only 30 cents per transaction plus 2.2 to 2.9 percent of each sale.

See Chapter 8 for a long list of other web sites at which you can sell your music.

Make free digital audio samples of your music available

Despite what you think of legal battles over the widespread sharing of digital music files, to sell more CDs online you have to make at least some of your music readily available ... for free. Getting fresh ears to experience your music is a battle. Don't put up obstacles by hoarding it all to yourself.

But you don't have to give away the whole store. Make at least three songs from your CD available in either MP3 or RealAudio formats, the most common digital forms. After fans hear your digital music samples, direct them where to go to buy your entire CD. Often, the easiest ways to make your song samples available are at the places where they can be purchased. For instance, CD Baby and Amazon can make digital samples a part of your sales page.

To summarize, your game plan for Internet CD sales should include:

1. Putting up an artist web site with a show schedule, CD sales page, photos and more
2. Encouraging fans to sign up for your free e-mail newsletter – then send monthly updates that are filled with your personality and strong sales offers
3. Having clear links to your online MP3 or RealAudio sound files so people can hear some of your sounds immediately
4. Making sure you have online ordering options available

Make appealing offers to your fans

When you have a new release and do a mailing to your fan list (whether in print or by e-mail), go beyond just saying, "Hey, we have a new CD. If you want it, send us money." Make a special offer. "Order within 10 days and get FREE shipping." "Buy one CD, get a second copy at half off to give to a friend." "The first 25 orders get autographed copies." Give your customers a real reason to buy more of your music NOW!

Use testimonials and positive quotes

Whether you're sending a sales message to fans or a plea to the media to cover you, don't just depend on your own words to make your point. Use quotes from satisfied fans, positive reviews or favorable comments from respected industry pros to back up your claims of worthiness. If more artists and record labels did this, they'd make more of an impression and sell a lot more releases.

Determine your sales goal and display it

If you don't choose a specific goal and make a commitment to it, chances are your actions will wither away quickly. To avoid this, write down your new action plan to double your CD sales and post it prominently on the wall of your office or rehearsal area. Look at this plan every day and affirm your dedication to achieving it.

Set a target number of units

To hit a target, you must be able to see the bull's-eye clearly. To reach your CD sales goals, you must have a number to aim for. First, determine your current level of sales. Let's say it's an average of 300 CDs a month.

In order to double your sales figures in 90 days, you'd have to sell 600 CDs a month or 1,800 units within the next three months. That's about 140 CD sales per week. Knowing these hard facts will focus your energies and allow you to know exactly where you stand.

Check your progress and adjust the plan as needed

As you head into the weeks leading through the next 90 days, measure your progress regularly. What's getting the best results? What's not working so well? How can you most effectively increase sales with a wise use of your current resources? What changes, if any, need to be made to reach the goal within 90 days?

Indie acts and labels around the world are selling hundreds and thousands of CDs every month. There's no reason you shouldn't be among their ranks right now!

High-Impact Promotional Strategies You Should Be Using to Market Your Music

Have you been in a marketing rut lately? Are you having a tough time coming up with new and innovative promotion ideas? You won't be for long. Soak up the ideas in this report and get moving. Every day that passes without you actively promoting your music is lost time. So read on ... then get busy!

Music Marketing and the State of Your Fans

In this first section, let's talk about sizzle and steak. You've most likely heard the old advertising credo "Sell the sizzle, not the steak." It's another way of saying "Push customer benefits, not product features." This mantra has been repeated time and time again in marketing circles for decades. Unfortunately, most people continue to ignore the wisdom.

To see how you stack up in this area, I'll give you a quick test. Answer these two questions: When it comes to communicating with your fans, what business are you in? And what do you really offer them?

If you answered, "I'm in the music business, and I offer them my CDs and live concerts," you're dead wrong. Items such as "music," "CDs" and "concerts" are pure features. And features are simply things you technically do or produce in the course of creating your music. Sure, you must focus on these things when you create them. But they're not what your fans focus on when they spend money on your recordings and live shows.

Question: So ... what *do* fans buy? Here's the answer (and write this down in a visible place and remind yourself of it often): The real reason consumers buy music is to experience the emotional and physical "state change" that occurs within them – because of the music you create. For instance ...

- High-energy music pumps up its followers and gets their adrenaline flowing.
- New Age and acoustic music soothes the minds and the bodies of listeners.
- Sad love songs remind romantic folks of a similar event in their lives.
- Ethnic music helps people connect with their roots.
- Oldies bring back memories and feelings of the good old days.
- Classical music awes and inspires.

Regardless of the style or genre, music touches people on both an emotional and physical level. The state of the listener before hearing your music is decidedly different from what it is during the hearing (or watching) of it. State changes add adventure and excitement to our lives – which is exactly why so many people turn to sex, drugs, alcohol and extreme sports to do the same thing for them.

Never forget this. And start asking yourself: What kind of state change does my music inspire in my fans? When you're creating, by all means focus on the music, the CDs and the concerts. But forget all that when it comes to communicating with your fans – and start concentrating on how your music affects people on a deeper level!

So when it comes to sending out marketing messages about your music, what's going to get the best response? Talking about your "new CD, now available at your favorite local record store"? Or reminding people of the real reason they're going to buy it? Meaning the emotional and physical payoff they get when they spend a few dollars or more on your music.

In case you didn't know it, you're no longer in the music business. You're now in the "state change" business – especially when it comes to marketing your music.

How to Use Pain and Pleasure to Promote Yourself

Let me ask you another question: What are the two major forces that motivate human beings to act? You might be tempted to say things like "money and sex" or "security and respect."

Yes, those are motivating factors, but let's break them down into the two most basic components. Here they are: Human beings either want to move closer to pleasure or away from pain. That's it. The motivation behind everything you or any other person does can be broken down into one or both of these categories: getting pleasure or avoiding pain.

Examples: Eating helps you avoid hunger pains and at times enjoy a fine meal (sorry, a Whopper doesn't count). You're inspired to make money to avoid the pain of not paying your bills and get the pleasure of treating yourself to the things you want.

Perhaps you play music to get the pleasure of creating music and the recognition that comes when you share it with others. Or maybe you play music to avoid the pain of not having an outlet for your creative urges.

Pleasure motivations occur when people aspire to a higher level or to experience one of those feel-good "state changes." Pain motivations occur when we want to eliminate a current physical or emotional nuisance, or when we want to avoid a potential loss we believe may happen in the near future.

Of these two motivators, pain is the strongest. People tend to grieve over a perceived loss more than a gain. For instance, which would be more intense: Your level of happiness at finding $100, or your level of frustration at losing $100? Most people would feel the loss more intensely.

Marketers use both of these factors all the time. For example, weight loss clinics and diet book publishers have two marketing options. One, they can concentrate on the pleasure people will get once they reach a desired lower weight. Or two, they can remind people how unhappy they are now and how that pain can be removed if they only sign up or buy the book. Of the two approaches, the second is the strongest motivator.

So how does this apply to marketing your music? Take a look at the emotional, physical and spiritual impact your music has on fans. Does it pump them up? Calm them down? Make them feel connected? Nostalgic? Romantic? Inspired? What's the real payoff your fans get from your music? By now you should know what that payoff is.

Now take those qualities and express them in both pleasure-gaining and pain-avoiding terms. Here are some examples:

A high-energy rock band

Pleasure: We'll get you pumped up and feeling alive and energetic.

Pain: Tired of your mundane nine-to-five work routine? Sick of sissy pop rock when you turn on the radio? We have the antidote for your blahs right here on our CD.

An acoustic pop-folk act

Pleasure: Our songs will soothe your mind with catchy, mellow guitar melodies and make you smile.

Pain: With your fast-paced schedule, the last thing you need is more of that angst-ridden grunge crap you always hear on the radio. Our music is your solution.

An avant-garde jazz trio

Pleasure: Exciting rhythms and invigorating instrumentation await you on our new CD. Give your ears the musical spice they hunger for.

Pain: Sure, you could continue to be lulled to sleep by the dull, predictable sounds of most new jazz acts. Or you could give yourself some much-deserved relief and treat yourself to real music from seasoned jazz pros.

A romantic balladeer

Pleasure: Snuggle up with your honey and sway to these timeless songs – guaranteed to supercharge your love life.

Pain: The recent slew of raw sex songs does more harm than good with your love life. The romantic relief you need awaits you on my new CD of soothing love songs.

Get the idea? Your best bet is to use both pain and pleasure tactics when writing your music marketing materials. Hit people from both angles. It will help drive home the benefits of your music and give your fans (and potential fans) one good reason after another to give your musical act a try... and keep coming back for more of the pleasure-gaining and pain-avoiding goodies you have waiting for them.

Identify your image

Bands that choose to portray a certain image often attempt to mislead the music-buying public. And these music consumers show their displeasure by staying away from your shows and new CDs in droves. Having an "image" implies something phony – a facade that tries to manipulate the people exposed to it.

Instead of trying to communicate your image, start marketing your "identity." An identity is an honest expression of what your music and personality are all about. I know this may seem like a nit-picking argument over semantics, since many people use these terms interchangeably. But if you focus on finding your "identity," it forces you to send a more honest message regarding your music.

And that kind of honesty breeds confidence and attracts fans like magnets.

Grab attention – with a purpose

Before you fall in love a crazy new promotion scheme, consider this: People will remember the most fascinating part of your marketing but not necessarily your band or new release. Of course, this all depends on what the most fascinating aspect is. If you display an eye-catching photo or piece of artwork on your ads or fliers, people may remember the visual image but not your band name. If you use a witty headline, they may remember the humor but not your musical identity.

Reality: Music consumers are first and foremost interested in the benefit they get from the artists they support. So if you want to interest them, relate your marketing pitch directly to their needs. And do it in a way that makes your band or new release the most fascinating part of the message.

For instance, the Tone Casualties label ran a print ad that still has me scratching my head. A collage of bizarre artwork takes up half of the ad, while small, "stylish" type that's hard to read is scattered about the other half. I think this ad is promoting several of the label's releases, but I'm not sure. I know that Tone Casualties specializes in unconventional, experimental sounds, but this experimental marketing ploy doesn't help get the message across.

A half-page ad from Hannibal Records, on the other hand, does a nice job of using humor to get its point made. The headline reads, "Did you hear the one about the Cuban piano player, the Tibetan nun and the Finnish accordionist?" The smaller subhead underneath explains, "It's no joke: They've made three must-have new world music albums for Hannibal." Each album then has a one-sentence description and that's it – short, sweet, interesting and effective.

Just like all good music marketing efforts should be!

Doing it yourself – at least at first – is better

According to John Huling, a New Age artist from Arizona, the personal approach is best. "If you see a store selling the type of music you play, immediately give the owner a copy of your album," says Huling in an issue of Disc Makers' *Fast Forward* newsletter. "Return a few days later to see if they liked it. If their response is positive, ask them to stock it."

Eventually, you'll get your release into enough stores and distributors will then be interested in taking on your line of recordings – thereby saving you a lot of time and effort dealing with so many different retailers. But in the meantime, as Huling points out, "the money from a lot of little stores does add up."

Huling also explains that the experience of releasing CDs on his own Novox record label greatly prepared him for being approached by major record companies. "I was offered a dollar per unit from one major label," he recalls. "There was no way I'd do that. But if I had not released my own albums and been successful as an independent artist, then those same offers would have sounded good."

Demo strategies that set your music apart

Whether you want to attract the attention of a publisher, record label, music magazine or radio station, you need to find ways to make your recorded submissions stand out. Here are two ideas few others are using:

1) A couple of years ago, as my staff and I were going through submissions to our annual music conference, we came across a short tape that featured snippets of about eight songs from one band. Each song faded out after about 30 seconds, and after a two-second pause, the next song began. We got a quick earful of this group's music without getting bored or having to fast-forward through the tape.

I believe that, in the right situations, this sampling presentation can be an effective one. It gives you more bang for your buck, especially if you make the recipient aware of the timesaving benefits of this format.

Strategy: Include a short letter that states something like: "You're busy. You haven't got time to listen to every note of every song that comes across your desk. That's why we've made it easy for you to enjoy a three-minute sampling of our six best songs. That's all it takes. Three minutes. And you're done. If you like what you hear, contact us for our full-length CD ..."

If more artists used this approach, they'd probably see a better response to unsolicited mailings.

2) This second demo submission technique could work well along with the first one or by itself. It involves recording a personalized voice message at the beginning of each CD you send. Let's say you plan to send the six-song sampler mentioned above. Make the first track a 30-second recording of your voice greeting the specific person the CD is meant for. Yes, this tactic will take a little extra time for you to burn individual CDs for each contact.

The CD should be delivered with a note saying: "I recorded a personal message just for you on the first 30 seconds of this CD. I think this is something you'll want to hear."

Once the person's curiosity is teased and he or she pops in the CD, your recorded message might say: "Hi, Pat. This is Fred from the band Green Slime. I really enjoy your columns in the Daily Music Rag, especially the piece you did on (insert any detailed reference, as long as it's genuine). I know you're busy and are probably sick of opening mail, so I thought I'd give you a change of pace with this voice cover letter. The rest of this disc contains... (here you can borrow wording used in the sampler CD example above)."

The reason these two tactics work is because they meet the two most important criteria for marketing music:

1) They keep the recipient's limited time foremost in mind, and

2) They are truly different from the norm.

Street Smarts

Here's a good example of a fresh angle for a compilation CD. Clay Dog Records put out *Street Dreams*, a collection of music from some of Chicago's more visible street musicians – recorded live at the corners and subway stops they frequent. **Lesson**: If you put together a compilation, make sure there's a logical and appealing thread that holds it all together. Saying "Here's a bunch of cool bands" won't cut it. But a lot of cool music centered around a common theme might sell.

The same thing goes for promoting a single artist. Always keep your image consistent. When people see your fliers, post cards, CD artwork or web site, they should know without a doubt that it's all coming from the same artist. You can do this by keeping your logo, typefaces and the tone of your wording consistent. This might seem bland and repetitious to the person designing the material. But always changing the look and feel of your marketing will simply confuse people.

What would you rather have: a lot of people who know exactly what your band is, or a lonely portfolio of disjointed press kits, photos and artwork?

College band payoff

The Dirges is a band made up of students attending Pennsylvania State University. The band's three independently released albums have sold a cumulative 10,000 copies in three years.

"Think about it," says guitarist/keyboardist Steve Bodner, "ten thousand people graduate from this college each year and move to places all across the country. We go right along with them."

Are you taking advantage of the college market?

Music promotion on wheels

Organic Records has a specially designed flatbed truck that travels city to city to get exposure for its artists. The acts can perform live right on the truck or simply give away samplers and promotional items from it at special events.

Can you develop a fresh method of exposing your music to new groups of people?

Sunny skies in the forecast

Artist Bryan Duncan released a new album called *Blue Skies*. To make the most of the album title, his record label ran radio spots sponsoring weather reports in key regions of the country. Duncan also did radio interviews during which he read the weather forecast on the air. You can bet there weren't many other artists taking this approach.

Is there anything about your CD title or band name that can be transformed into a creative marketing strategy?

Cover up

Tired of being denied radio airplay because stations prefer to pump out familiar music to the masses? One solution: Stop fighting and go with the status quo. Australian band the Clouds received some attention when it recorded a cover of Glen Campbell's "Wichita Lineman."

"It's a beautiful song," says bassist Patricia Young. "Not only that, it's a lot easier to pick up airplay with familiar material."

Might there be a cover song that you can put your own fresh spin on?

Thinking outside the box: On a recent trip to the library, I checked out Jay Levinson's book *Guerrilla Marketing Attack*. Like the other books in Levinson's "Guerrilla" series, this volume is packed with dozens of usable business-building tactics. I've taken the liberty of giving some of the concepts from the book a musical slant with the following four tips.

Use eight stamps instead of one

As you know, people are bombarded with mail. Music editors, program directors, managers, distributors – they all receive an avalanche of unsolicited mail. One creative, low-cost way to make your package stand out is to use more stamps than anyone else is using. Instead of sending your letter with a single first-class stamp, why not stick on several stamps that all add up to 37 cents? Who would fail to open a letter with eight stamps on it? You might even write a funny phrase like "We're hoping for your stamp of approval" on the outside of the envelope.

Don't ask fans to join a mailing list – ask them to become a member of your club

Based on the headline above, I'm sure you can already see the difference between being added to a list and becoming a member of a special club. Signing up on a list is cold and impersonal. Joining a club is warm and cozy.

Advice: Put together an inexpensive package that might include a membership certificate with the person's name on it, a fan club card, an autographed photo, free sampler CD, button and any other fun trinkets you can find at discount stores.

If people join the club while at one of your shows, you can either give them all of this cool stuff then or let them know you'll mail a package to them soon afterward. Then make sure and send it as soon as possible, and follow up with regular newsletters and updates.

Research has shown that when you give free things to people, they are much more receptive and likely to spend money on you in the near future. The rule here is simple: To reap the rewards of your labor on the back end, you have to give something away and keep your customers' needs foremost in mind on the front end. That's what effective marketing is all about!

Arrange for positive picketers to demonstrate

The idea here is to gather a group of your supporters to demonstrate outside of an establishment. But instead of protesting, these people would carry signs that praise your music or new release. Each sign would have a different review quote, ringing endorsement or photo.

This marketing tactic is so fresh and unexpected, it just might generate a lot of favorable publicity in the area. You'd be wise to get the blessings of the club manager or storeowner before proceeding with this one. But with the potential exposure it could generate, you should have no problem finding at least one establishment to actively participate in the mock picket.

Embrace your customers for a lifelong relationship

Most music marketers don't see the ongoing value of a single customer. They sell a new fan a $12 CD and take pride in making a $9 or $10 profit. But the guerrilla music marketer sees it differently.

He or she knows that with proper care and attention, a single new fan can be worth far more over the course of many years. Not only will that fan buy future releases and attend numerous shows, but this person will also tell others about this great artist that treats him or her so well.

These new, referred fans will also buy a lot of CDs and pay the cover at many live concerts. A single CD sale (with a $10 profit) has the potential to be worth 10 to 20 times that over several years. That is, if you caress and pamper your fans (figuratively, of course) and show them you really care.

The Easiest Way to Make Money in the Music Business: Create Multiple Streams of Income

Most likely, you've been performing regularly, attracting some new fans, selling a few CDs and generally having a good time making music. In many ways, you're already successful and deserve to feel good about you're accomplishments. But there's also a good chance you have a nagging sense of deficiency. More specifically, financial deficiency. You're not alone. It seems the majority of people who pursue creative passions aren't making the Big Bucks.

Even though this is a common situation for music people, that doesn't mean you should mindlessly accept it as a permanent state of being. There are ways to increase the flow of money into your life through music. The best method that successful artists use to create wealth is developing "multiple streams of income." The idea here is that small streams of cash from several different sources can eventually build into a steady, flowing river of revenue.

Recently, I read Barbara Winter's insightful book *Making a Living Without a Job*, in which she discusses "multiple profit centers." Winter writes: "Rather than thinking in terms of having a single source of income (as we are trained to do when we see our income tied to a job), the savvy entrepreneur thinks about developing several income sources. With planning – and an openness to additional opportunities as they come along – you can create as many streams as you desire."

To illustrate the point, Winter mentions Richard Branson, the founder of Virgin Records, who reportedly oversees more than 150 different small enterprises (when he's not ballooning around the globe, that is). And Branson keeps inventing new projects all the time.

Don't think you have to run an international corporation to make this tactic work. If we simply look at the standard ways an artist can earn income, this multiple profit center approach becomes clear.

A musical act can potentially make money from:

1. Live performance fees

2. CD sales at live shows

3. CD sales through distributors and retail stores

4. CD sales through mail order catalogs

5. Merchandise sales at gigs (and each piece of merchandise is a separate profit center)

6. CD and merchandise sales on the Internet

7. Song placement in films and television

8. Fees from licensing your songs, name and image

9. Mechanical royalties on CD sales

10. Performance rights royalties

And these are just some of the ways.

Bottom line: The key to making a decent living with music lies in making sure that the many streams available to you are producing. Expecting only your income from live shows or only your money from retail CD sales to bring in a sufficient amount is risky at best. It's a lot easier, for instance, to generate $500 a month each from five different (but related) sources than it is to pray that one source will reel in the whole $2,500.

These multiple streams of income aren't limited to activities that involve your songs or band. What other skills and opportunities do you possess that you could leverage into extra cash? Can't think of any? Try again. Believe me, everyone has the potential to generate additional revenue – if he or she only searches for possibilities.

For example, let's say you have a basement full of recording gear that you've turned into a quality home studio. Perhaps you use it to record your own band or solo projects and are now ready to offer your services to earn extra cash.

Of course, the obvious thing to do is make your services available to record other bands and songwriters who are looking for good, inexpensive recordings of their music. And many people with home recording setups do just that. The only problem is, that's all they do ... accept to complain that not enough paying customers are booking time.

The trick is to look outside the normal, predictable methods. To demonstrate this philosophy, here are 11 random ideas on how a person with a home studio could create multiple profit centers:

1. Copyright registration service

It seems everyone is confused about how to register a copyright with the Library of Congress. It's not really that difficult, but many of your studio clients may pay you a fee to do it for them and save them the trouble.

2. Recording classes

Do you feel competent enough to effectively share your knowledge of the recording process with others? If so, offer basic recording classes in your studio.

3. CD duplication

People who use your recording services are prime candidates for CD duplication. Offer that additional service to your customers and reap the rewards.

4. Voice-overs and spoken word

Music is not the only way to make money with a home recording studio. You can also reach out to customers who need to record voice-overs for radio commercials and instructional multi-media projects, as well as poets and authors wanting to produce spoken-word recordings of their work.

5. Soundtrack library

Many tech-savvy musicians make extra money recording instrumental tracks that are used in the background of films, TV shows, video games, computer-based training materials and more.

6. Compilation CDs

Most of your music customers are going to want to get their songs exposed after they have a finished product. Once you have a list of satisfied clients, offer to release a compilation CD of the best acts. The bands pay you a fee per song (perhaps $50 to $75 a minute) to put it all together. As long as the total fees you collect are more than your costs, you come out ahead – while helping a lot of bands get the notoriety they crave.

7. Equipment rental

I know, you would never think of parting with your new, expensive gear – even for a few hours. But surely, you have some equipment in your arsenal that you'd be comfortable renting to someone. This way, he or she gets to use the component for a reasonable fee, and you end up with an extra income source.

8. Audio birthday cards

Offer a special service whereby paying customers come in and record a personal greeting to a loved one. You could promote it as being a much more appealing gift than a typical, boring greeting card.

9. Audio restoration

Are you good with digital audio editing software? If so, find customers who need to restore old vinyl albums or want to convert scratchy analog audio programs to CD.

10. Mastering

Recording individual song tracks is just one part of the process. Before a full CD is replicated, all of the tracks need to be mastered so the whole collection has a cohesive, high-quality sound. Teach your customers the importance of mastering and offer that as an added source of income.

11. Morning radio show jingles and song parodies

I know this one can work because I've done it. A few years ago there was a local morning show team that paid me $100 to $200 a month to write and record song parodies and goofy jingles for them. It wasn't a huge amount of money, but it helped fill some financial gaps – and it was quite fun!

No matter where your special niche in the music business lies, there are literally dozens of related ways to earn extra cash. In her book, Winter suggests not trying to launch all your new money-making ideas at one time. Pick the one you're most passionate about and get it going first. Once it's up and running, begin another profit center. Then another. Before long, you'll have a good number of these revenue centers working for you.

Over time, however, you'll find some of your activities losing steam (or yourself losing interest) and it'll be time to drop them. That's why it's a good idea to always be thinking of new income-producing concepts.

In his book, *No More Cold Calls*, marketing expert Jeffrey Lant describes building what he calls the "mobile mini-conglomerate" – another phrase for this multi-pronged way of earning a living.

He suggests some of the following tactics for regularly developing new moneymaking opportunities:

Keep an idea file

Whether it's in a notebook, file folder, shoebox or on your computer, have one designated place where you store all of your ideas for making extra money. This will pay big dividends and ensure that you don't lose or forget your best ideas.

Keep an expert file

Whenever you meet someone who may be able to help you in the pursuit of a moneymaking venture, make sure to ask for his or her name and contact info. This especially goes for people and companies with whom you might be able to work out lucrative cross-promotions.

Collect articles, books and publications about money

In addition to music-related publications, make sure and expose yourself to a variety of titles on marketing and making money. As you read about success stories in other industries, always ask yourself: "How can this good idea be applied to my interests and skills in the music business?"

Get a brainstorming partner

While you want to train your mind to be on the lookout for new opportunities, working by yourself all the time has its limitations. That's where having a brainstorming partner or two comes in handy. Ask your most creative and open-minded associates to join you in a think session, in which the main topic is coming up with new money-making ideas. You may be pleasantly surprised with the workable concepts that pop up during these meetings.

Keep records of what did and didn't work

Creating another income steam can be exciting and challenging. But if the new profit center isn't producing, you'll just be spending your limited time and energy in vain. Keep a log of your start-up expenses, specific actions taken and the bottom-line results of your efforts. Use this information to determine whether the new income stream is worth continuing.

If you're completely satisfied with your current income level, congratulations. You're in a select group. But if there's any discontent regarding your finances, the multiple-streams approach may be the best answer to help you overcome a cash-flow deficiency.

7 Crucial Music Marketing Steps You Need to Be Taking Right Now

When I originally wrote this article, it ran in January as a motivational message to help music people formulate their New Year's resolutions. But the advice contained here is timeless.

Regardless of what month you read this, think of it as a starting point for the next 12 months. And ask yourself: How will the next 12 months be even better than the last 12? What steps will I take to make sure my music reaches even more ears over the next year? And how can I make sure I prosper accordingly?

Here are my best suggestions for powerful marketing ideas and tactics you should adopt right now:

1) Commit to spending 10 minutes a day on promoting your music

I was flipping through John Kremer's great book, *1001 Ways to Market Your Books*, and came across a particularly inspiring section. Even though this resource was written for authors and book publishers, his advice on spending a small amount of time every day on marketing can easily be adapted to music. Therefore, I've taken two of Kremer's paragraphs and altered them so they apply to you:

"Ten minutes a day – really, that's all it takes. Mail a letter. Send out a press release. Phone someone. Fire off an e-mail note. It need not require much time – 10 minutes is enough – but it can make a world of difference on how well your music sells. I don't want any more excuses. If your music hasn't sold or you haven't landed many gigs, there is only one reason – provided the music has any merit to begin with. And the reason is: You're just plain lazy. If you spend only 10 minutes a day – every day – on every CD you release and every show you book, you will generate an incredible momentum for your music.

"There is no reason why any of your CDs should die after six weeks in the marketplace. Album releases, like diamonds, are forever – that is, if you're willing to put a little elbow grease behind their promotion and use those 10 minutes a day wisely."

Thanks again to John Kremer for those hard-hitting words of wisdom. Can you find 10 short minutes a day to work on exposing your music? Now would be a great time to start doing just that. Your future in music literally depends on it.

2) Make certain that every time you engage in a music marketing activity, you have a specific objective in mind

While spending those 10 minutes a day will deliver tremendous benefits, you'll get twice the results if you focus on the purpose of each activity. Simply getting someone on the phone or sending a letter is great, but for what purpose are you communicating? Begging an editor for a review or a club owner for a gig will lead to press clippings and live shows, but having a fresh and detailed slant to your pitch will yield far more exposure.

Example: Let's say that March is National Fire Prevention Month (I don't believe it actually is, but just play along) and one of your band members is a volunteer fire fighter. You're also aware of a local children's hospital that has a special unit for burn victims. Contact a local club and discuss the concept of a charity show, with proceeds going to the burn unit. Once it's set up, contact area editors to inform them of the event and pitch a story idea that ties in with your musician firefighter.

You can even take this idea further by asking a local pizza chain to provide free food during a pre-show party the night of the concert. The pizza place would benefit by being associated with such a worthy event. You should also allow them to distribute coupons that night. In return, they promote the benefit concert at all of their locations during the weeks leading up to it.

Which do you think would be more effective? The specific, focused approach? Or just asking "Hey, can you give us a gig?"

3) Connect with your fans, the media and industry contacts at least once every two months

People are bombarded with more information and demands today than at any time in human history. As much as we like to think our music contacts sit around and think about us often, this simply isn't true. Whether they are fans, media people or industry big shots, they have to be reminded at regular intervals that we are still there.

Your solution: Put together an informational post card (good) or amusing newsletter (better) and mail it out at least once every two months. Actually, your fans should hear from you by e-mail at least once a month. Whatever you send out, make sure the mailing piece attempts to inspire some kind of action from the recipient – coming to a show, ordering your CD or new T-shirt, calling you for more info, etc.

4) Develop a Fan-Focused PR Mindset

Being a successful self-promoting musician is a way of life and a manner of thinking that you must carry with you at all times. It's more than just a dream of some day being rich and famous. In fact, becoming rich and famous should not even be your primary goal. Your focus must be on creating great music and getting it into the ears of as many fans as possible. Fame and fortune are merely byproducts of being a good self-promoter consistently over the long haul.

Developing a fan-focused PR mindset means that your brain is always ready and eager to recognize exposure opportunities. And you don't limit your search for ideas to the obvious music sources. Every thing, person and place you encounter is a potential marketing opportunity. From now on, view everything through the lens of "Is there anything here I can use to promote my music?"

Most musicians wander through their careers with blinders on. The only circumstance they recognize and talk about is how difficult it can be to get exposure. Don't fall into this negative tunnel-vision trap. Instead, program your mind to seek out PR possibilities at every turn. Make it your mission to build a growing army of fans by any means necessary.

Your goal is to reach a critical mass – whereby fans of your musical genre hear about you repeatedly from multiple sources: on a radio talk show, during a TV news broadcast, in a music review column, on a best-selling sales chart online, in a specialized retail outlet and more.

With a fan-focused PR mindset, I guarantee you'll find exposure opportunities popping up all around you.

5) Determine Your Specific Musical Identity

Not long ago I wrote a book called *Branding Yourself Online*. The book isn't specifically about the music business, but the principles I spell out in it can and should be applied to your music marketing efforts. The basic thrust of the book is that people can become brand names in the same way that companies and products can.

Some of the best examples of individuals who have branded themselves include Oprah Winfrey, Martha Stewart, Rush Limbaugh and Howard Stern. Most likely, the mere mention of each name conjures up a specific identity in your mind. Love them or hate them, you know immediately who they are, what they do and the unique way that they do it.

So how can you apply this principle to yourself and your music? As you may have guessed, telling people that you're a singer-songwriter or that you play in a rock and roll band won't help you promote yourself effectively. A million musicians are saying the same thing. You need to be more specific in order to occupy a unique space in people's minds.

Saying you play "rockabilly songs for car lovers" or "accordion music for gardeners," as pigeonholed as those phrases may seem, does a better job of giving you a well-defined identity.

To help you discover your musical niche, do some soul searching and examine who you are as a person and a musician. Answer these questions: What motivates you? What themes come up in your songs most often? What impression of you do fans get when they hear your recordings or see you perform?

Look over your answers and determine if there's a common trait that runs through them. If not, you must choose a specific aspect of your many characteristics and commit to making that the focus of your brand image.

You can't be all things to all people. Therefore, I highly encourage you to pick one characteristic of your musical persona and exaggerate it – then use that angle as your primary identity.

Remember, your goal is to have music fans mentally link your name to the brand identity you choose. Once established, brand identities are hard to change, so make sure the identity you choose is the best one for you.

6) Think Niche

Most songwriters and musicians hate to be labeled or categorized in any way. You probably feel the same way. That's understandable. You're a creative being, and you want to be free to express yourself in all kinds of ways. Unfortunately, what's good for the muse isn't always what's best for the self-promoter.

The best way to attract a loyal following fast is to specialize. As I mentioned earlier, you can't be all things to all people. If your image, style or selection of songs is too watered down, you leave nothing for most music fans to latch onto.

Singer-songwriter Brad Belt offers a good example of what I'm talking about. For several years, he had a ho-hum career as a middle-of-the-road pop songwriter. A couple of years ago, Brad attended a songwriting workshop and was struck with one piece of advice: Write songs about topics you love.

Since he's an avid golfer, Brad wrote a humorous song about playing the game. His golfing pals responded positively. So he wrote another funny, golf-related song.

And another. After a while he had enough golf songs to put out an entire CD of tunes about the sport.

The results? Brad held a CD release party at a local country club and sold more than $800 worth of CDs in one night. He later put together a string of live performances at golf courses and country clubs throughout his region. By narrowing his focus and filling a niche, Brad has more fans and more recognition than he had when he wrote pop songs for a mass audience.

The thing is, Brad can still write and perform some regular pop songs and exercise his versatility. But keeping his primary identity as the funny-golf-songs guy, he makes more of an impact.

What topics do you love writing and singing about? What niche can you fill? And, most importantly, with what identity can you have the most impact?

7) Be patient when waiting for results

So, you start living up to these resolutions. You're spending at least 10 minutes a day on promotion, communicating with people regularly, focusing on fans and marketing yourself with passion. Six months go by and … Hey, where's the fame and fortune? Baker lied to me!

Here I go overstating the obvious again, but all good things take time. It takes time for people to finally get what you're about, to recognize your name, to show any support for your music. Cherish the small victories and know that greater success will be yours if you persist. It's happened many thousands of times to artists around the world. Those who have a burning desire and definite purpose withstand the obstacles and come out on top.

Sadly, many of the ones who fail give up right as they're on the brink of success. They'll never realize how close they actually came to making a good living doing something they love. But you'll be different because you're going to persist until you get to where you want to be.

There's a warm, fuzzy thought as you head into the next 12 months of your life and career. If you truly put these resolutions to work, I guarantee the coming year will be even more fruitful than the last one.

25 Tips to Help You Market Your Music Through the Mail

Sure, you use e-mail, have a fax, carry a cell phone or use a digital pager. Maybe you also have a web site and use a Blackberry. Taking advantage of modern technology to market your music is fine and dandy, but somewhere in your promotional bag of tricks you'd better be using direct mail.

Yes, I know it's an old marketing method and people keep saying they're sick of "junk mail." But the truth is: Direct mail still works – if you know what you're doing. That's why I'm dedicating this entire report to the topic. Here is a list of 25 techniques you can use to make sure your direct mail efforts pay off.

1) Come up with a short, easy-to-remember name for your record label or music catalog

There's a moving and hauling business not far from my house called Two Men and a Truck. You can't get more basic than that, but what a great name. There can be no doubt as to what service this firm provides. Who would you rather hire? Two Men and a Truck or Smith Hauling Services?

To use a more specific musical reference, which of these names conjures up a more defined image: Zoo Entertainment or Metal Blade Records? I realize it's hip these days to come up with an obscure term and then try to build it into a recognizable "brand name." Personally, I don't have the time or the money it takes to educate the public. I'd much rather call my mail order device the All Power Pop Music Catalog than something silly like Gum Drops.

2) Use short, benefit-rich sentences to hook media people and fans into reading your mailing piece

Craft your words so they're quick and lively – and full of zest. And put the emphasis on the interests of the person receiving your mailing piece. Go through the document and count the number of times the word "I" is used. Then count the number of times the word "you" pops up. There should be at least twice as many you's as there are I's. If not, you need to rewrite.

Believe me, you can almost always turn an "I" sentence into a "you" sentence. Examples: "I'd really like to get a feature story in your magazine" should be transformed into something like "Many of your readers are hungry for info on local metal bands, and ours is one of the more prominent acts in the region."

"I'll send our new CD soon" can be turned into "You'll receive our new CD as soon as it comes out."

3) Avoid over-hyped, pie-in-the-sky claims in your literature

Don't try to fool people with remarkable claims, unless they are truly based on something tangible. I'm tired of reading idiotic lines such as "the Blah Blah Band is ready to take over the world." Keep your marketing materials upbeat – but also keep at least one foot in the real world. People can spot deceptive, overblown claims from miles away.

4) When you advertise, use the two-step method to generate a growing list of potential buyers

In most cases, you shouldn't try to make a direct sale from an ad. Offer a free catalog or sampler CD for little or no money (perhaps just a dollar or a self-addressed stamped envelope). Once you have a list of prospects who responded to your ad, you can follow up by mail as often as you like with stronger sales offers.

5) Offer a strong guarantee to fans

Let's assume you have a lot of faith in the quality of the music on your CDs. (And if you don't have faith in it, you're in trouble.) Why not offer a 30-day, 90-day or one-year guarantee? Most indie musicians offer no guarantee at all. People are slow enough to take a chance on buying new music, out of fear of wasting their money. So why not give your customers the extra feeling of security? Surprisingly, marketing studies have shown that the longer the guarantee period, the fewer the returns.

6) Set aside a regular time for brainstorming new marketing ideas and ways to serve your fans better

Buy a notebook or journal and start capturing your ideas on paper. It doesn't have to be a fancy, flowery journal. A 39-cent spiral notebook from Walgreens will do just fine, as long you use it to record all of your new ideas for getting the word out and reaching new fans. You need to constantly improve what you offer.

7) Consider writing a short manual with step-by-step details on how to break into your musical niche

Surely, there are people who would love to know how to do what you do. There are several books already available on how to break into the music business. But what about a booklet on how to become a successful acoustic solo act? Or rap artist? Or jingle writer? Or regional booking agent? Or reggae promoter?

It doesn't have to be a hard cover bestseller. A simple stapled booklet or plastic comb-bound number made up at your local printer will do just fine. You can not only sell the book by mail and online to create a little extra cash flow, but it will likely stir up some positive publicity for you (and your music). And by including an offer to contact you in the booklet, it will also act as a customer-generating tool. So start writing.

8) Put a priority on managing your growing list of buyers, prospects and media contacts

It's easy to let things slip through the cracks. But when you get sloppy with orders and information requests from prospective fans and interested media folks, you're asking for trouble. You need to have a system (preferably a computer database file) in which you enter all of your customer and media information – including where each originated and what buyers have purchased from you in the past.

9) Collect music ads and direct mail pieces you feel are especially effective

Save them in a swipe file and refer to them for inspiration when creating any new ads or mailings for yourself. Don't copy directly from them. Instead, borrow the best concepts and put your own personal spin on them.

10) Always include "address correction requested" just under your return address

People move all the time. Addresses change. If you mail first class, the post office will forward the mail to a person's new address for one year. That's great, but you'll have an outdated address in your files and your offer will be delayed getting to its destination. If you send bulk mail and a person has moved, the post office will simply trash your mailing piece. They won't forward bulk mail.

However, if you typeset "address correction requested" on the front panel, they will send you the current address (or alert you that the person has moved with no forwarding address). There is a small fee for this service with bulk mail; there is no charge for corrections when mailing first class. And it's worth it, since it keeps you from continuing to pay for mail that ends up in the Dead Letter Office.

11) Handle customer complaints immediately

I know, it's tempting to put off calling back that irate fan who still hasn't received your new CD. You can call him tomorrow ... or when it's not so busy ... or when you're in a better mood. Stop making excuses and deal with the problem now. Solve a complaint quickly and you'll have a satisfied fan for life.

12) Emphasize a deadline – a date by which the prospect must respond to get a special price or other perk

Most people are slow to act – even when the action they need to take is in their best interest. Create some motivation by offering a reduced price or extra freebie if they order by a specific date within the next couple of weeks.

13) Emphasize a limited quantity

Using scarcity will also motivate people. In essence, you're saying, "Here are some goodies I have that are yours for the taking – but only if you're one of the first 50 people to place an order. Act quickly or you will lose out."

14) Offer a free bonus or free shipping with a minimum dollar amount

Reward customers who spend more money with you. For instance, in my catalogs I used to make the offer: "FREE shipping in the U.S. on orders of $75 or more." You can also offer a free button, CD or other product with every order over a certain amount.

15) Use personalized letters

Sending out generic pitches to your buyers and media contacts is fine. But you can triple the impact by taking the time to personalize each mailing piece. For instance, in a cover letter you would not only include the person's name, you would also make a reference specific to his or her needs.

Example: "I see you recently purchased my debut CD. Thanks so much for your support. I wanted you to be the first to know that I just released a new CD of fresh folk songs. As a previous customer, you might be interested in getting your own copy at a special price."

16) Use a P.S. on every letter

The headline is supposed to be the most-read part of any ad or sales letter. The P.S. portion of a letter is the second most read. Use this powerful tool to restate the main points made in the body of the letter and ask for the order (or for the media person to contact you).

17) Save money by designing an order form into your sales letter

If you're on a slim budget or don't need an elaborate mailing package, you can make your sales letter do double duty. Put your offer in the top three-quarters of the letter. Use the bottom panel as a "clip and mail (or fax)" order form, complete with a broken-border cut line.

Tip: You can also put your web address and phone number inside the order form for customers who would rather call or order online.

18) Track the results of every ad you run and every mailing piece you send

When you really start using direct mail effectively, you may have dozens of ads running and many offers being sent out. You need to keep track of where the best responses are coming from. You can do that by inserting a special code in each ad or mailer. Then calculate the results to discover your most lucrative methods.

19) Stay aware of what your competition is offering and how they are positioning themselves

I don't believe you need to have a "kill the competition" attitude to succeed. It's an abundant world, and there's plenty for everyone to get a piece of the pie. But you do need to be aware of how others in your genre are marketing themselves. This awareness helps you adjust and keep your unique position in the minds of customers.

20) Find out what the shipping charges are for every new (especially heavy) item you offer

Do this so you can add the appropriate shipping fee to the customer's final total. For instance, the cost to ship a sweatshirt runs more than the fee to ship a single CD. You don't want to overcharge your customers, and you don't want to short-change yourself by losing money on shipping fees.

21) Keep in mind that five times as many people read a headline as read the body of an ad or sales piece

That's exactly what advertising guru David Ogilvy and many other experts have said. Therefore, you should: 1) Use a headline, and 2) Make sure it speaks directly to the recipients' interests and carries impact.

Example: Songwriter and comedian Greg Tamblyn uses this headline at the top of his flier: "Saving the World from Whiny Victim Love Songs." It grabs attention and ties into his funny, positive persona.

22) Ship orders quickly

It's easy to get sidetracked. But just think of your own expectations when you order something by mail. Usually, you can't wait to get your hands on it. Your customers are no different. So send off all orders right away.

23) Consider either including shipping fees in your prices or listing the fees next to each individual item in your catalog

The idea here is to make doing business with you easy. Some catalogs require knowledge of Calculus to complete the order form. Simplify the work your customers have to do and they'll reward you by buying more of what you offer.

24) Bundle your CDs, T-shirts, buttons, coffee mugs and more into mega-packages for serious buyers

Having a variety of related products and services to sell is great. If potential buyers don't care for one item, they'll hopefully find others listed in your direct mail offering that they can use. But for those free-spending, hard-core customers, it's wise to put together special package deals that deliver a big dose of your music stuff all at once. It's a win-win. Your fans save money by buying in bulk – and you end up richer in the process.

25) Send check orders right away

Some companies like to wait until checks clear before fulfilling orders. I suggest you send the merchandise right away. The quick service to honest customers will create enough good will to offset the occasional bad check.

Exceptions: When the name and address on the check is different than the ship-to name and address. When in doubt, you can either call the customer directly or ask your bank to verify that it is an active account.

As you can see from this list, there are many ways to make direct-mail marketing more profitable. So in addition to your other promotional plans, be sure to add at least a little snail mail into the mix.

Advertising Your Music: How to Make It Pay (and Avoid the Most Common Mistakes)

Whether you've spent thousands of dollars on four-color ads in national magazines or just $50 to place a small ad in your local music rag, chances are you've paid to advertise your music at one time or another. Get used to it. The more successful your band or record label becomes, the more likely it'll be that you'll steer some of your promotional budget into ad dollars.

Most bands and record labels quickly slap together an ad at the last minute and run with it – all the while feeling good that they are "advertising" their music. Others go crazy with cutting-edge artwork or a quirky idea that amuses the band members. But do these ads serve the real purpose for advertising in the first place?

To be effective, your ads need to plant your name and identity into the minds of music consumers (or industry types, if you're advertising in a trade paper). If it doesn't accomplish that, it's dead weight. Your ads need to make compelling offers and inspire people to take action to hear or buy your music. If it doesn't, you're simply spending money to stroke your ego instead of get results.

Here are my thoughts on a few print ads I found while flipping through some national music magazines. Just for fun, I rated each one on a scale from 1 to 10. I hope these critiques inspire you to start getting a lot more bang for your advertising buck.

Tooth & Nail Records ran a full-page, four-color ad in *Alternative Press* to promote 11 of its releases. The page had the label name at the top, all 11 album covers with band names, titles and formats listed. Tooth & Nail's address, phone number and web site were displayed at the bottom.

I suppose if your recordings are distributed to retail outlets, you don't want to rub store owners the wrong way by being too blatant about asking for direct sales from consumers in ads – even though direct sales are more profitable for you. You can gain more clout with distributors by backing up your CDs with "national advertising." But if you encourage buyers to make purchases from you instead of them, why should the stores bother?

I'm certain that's the case with Tooth & Nail – and if so, this ad performs its marketing function while also including enough contact info for serious fans to reach the label directly. However, if your label were not relying heavily on retail distribution for sales, this ad would provide only generic "image" promotion – a bad move for a record company on a tight budget.

Ad rating: 8

A full-page ad for Grand Royal doesn't fare as well. It features some cool artwork and graphics, but the ad is quite confusing to my eyes. The phrases "Josephine Wiggs Experience" and "Bon Bon Lifestyle" appear in the top half of the ad. If you're already familiar with this record label's artists, you might have some idea of what's going on. If you're not, you'd be inclined to ask, "Which one is the band name and which is the album title?" Then the name "Moistboyz" is typeset down below with the words "In Stores Now." This ad creates more head scratching than sales potential in my mind. Grand Royal does include its web site in the ad but no address or phone number.

Ad rating: 4

(An ad from Sub Pop Records reveals a great way to avoid the confusing band name vs. album title dilemma. The ad has the band names in bold type and the titles in quotation marks. There should be no doubt if you use this format.)

Here's a great one: A full-page ad from Grass Records. The powers that be at this label took songs from 10 of their artists and put together a 20-song sampler CD. Then they put it on sale at Best Buy for only $1.99. (Great strategy: Get the music into people's ears cheap up front, then make your money on the back end through future sales.) The ad points out that each sampler CD contains a $3 mail-in rebate good towards the purchase of any full-length Grass Records CD. Of course, those titles are also available at Best Buy.

The ad then shows four of those full-length album covers with blurbs from the press under each one describing the music. You should know I'm a big fan of marketers who let consumers know what kind of music a band plays. The ultra-hip labels might like to shroud their ads in mystery, but the bands and labels that clearly communicate and provide sales incentives are the ones that come out on top.

(This should go without saying, but here it is anyway: Of course, the music has to be good and meaningful for most artists to succeed. Okay, I feel better now.)

The Grass Records ad ends with a plea to contact the label and join its fan club. Web site, toll-free 800 number and address options are provided. All the ingredients are here for a very effective ad.

Ad rating: 9

The first time I glanced at the full-page ad from Re-Construction/Cargo Music, I had serious doubts. Graphically, it was far too busy – even for an ad that promoted industrial and sythcore acts. Lots of various, disjointed artwork and type mashed together in an uninviting visual stew. But upon closer examination, it fared much better.

What I liked most about this ad were the descriptions of each act. Not only did they describe the music, but most weren't squeamish about making comparisons to other bands (example: "… should appeal to fans of Cop Shoot Cop and Filter"). When introducing yourself to the public through ads, don't be afraid to give people a point of reference. The small type at the bottom of this ad did ask fans to write for a free catalog. Address and web site info were included.

Ad rating: 6

Epitaph Records' half-page, black and white ad in the *Illinois Entertainer* scored some points. First, the headline of the ad reads "You scratch my back and I'll STAB YOURS." That's clever and attention getting. Second, the ad promoted the Epitaph Hotline, which you could call to hear song samples of any of the five bands shown in the ad. Now there's a fresh way of getting people to hear new music by only risking a long-distance phone call. When you call to hear the music samples, I assume that complete ordering info is provided (since no other contact info is included in the ad).

Now here are some problems with the ad: There are no descriptions whatsoever of the bands' music. Sure, the hotline is there so I can find out for myself, but I'd be a lot more inclined to call if I knew that some of this music was similar to stuff I already like. Sorry, but the backstabbing reference in the headline doesn't quite narrow it down. Also, the hotline is mentioned in relatively small type at the bottom of the ad – almost as an afterthought. It should be the primary focus of the ad, especially since few other labels are doing it.

Ad rating: 7

To wrap up this report, here are a few principles you should use to generate better results from your advertising efforts:

Have a purpose for every ad

If you're running an ad just because everyone else is, or because you have a new release coming out and it's the thing to do … slow down. Beyond that, what's your real objective for advertising? Is it to get people to go to stores and buy your new CD? Add people to your mailing list? Solicit mail order sales of your recordings? Promote a live show?

Don't expect an ad to work miracles and accomplish multiple objectives. Pick one purpose for each ad. Then make sure its design works toward that end.

Remain consistent with your theme and design

Choose a look and attitude that will stay the same for many weeks and months to come. Having a consistent design and feel to your ads burns an impression of your music into the minds of consumers. And that's exactly what you want to do!

Think of the Coca-Cola logo. It's changed very little over the decades. And it's one of the most recognized images in the world. Bottom line: Consistency rules!

Start small

Don't think your ads have to be bigger than the other guy's or gal's. A lot of marketers let their egos steer their ad decisions, not rational thought. A series of small ads run regularly over time will have 10 times the impact of one or two full-blown, full-page ads that people never see again.

Make the offer prominent in your ad

After you decide on the marketing objective for your ad, create a corresponding offer that will inspire readers to take action. Examples: a free catalog, a $3 discount, free CDs for the first 50 people, etc. Then make sure that offer is prominent in your ad. Don't bury it like some of the ads mentioned earlier.

Stick with a budget

Figure out how much per month or per quarter you can budget for advertising and then stick to your plan. There are two reasons to do this: 1) So you don't go nuts and blow your whole bank roll on advertising, and 2) So you don't get side-tracked and skip advertising when you need to be. As you may know, I don't think you always have to be running display ads. But during those months when it's in your best interest, make sure there's a system in place so you don't miss publication deadlines and lose out on the exposure.

Include complete contact info

There's no excuse for leaving out your address, phone, fax, e-mail and web site info. If you have them, list them!

Before you rush to slap together another ad, turn to this report and look over these tips. You'll be glad you did.

This Book Is Just One Part of an Ongoing Music Career Adventure

I hope your decision to read this book marks the beginning of a lengthy and successful journey. I'm confident that the principles and suggestions in this book will inspire you and help boost your self-promotion efforts to new levels. But the transaction shouldn't end there.

To make sure these ideas stick, I encourage you to visit my web site at **TheBuzzFactor.com**. There you'll find free articles and dozens of resources to help you get exposure, book more gigs, attract fans and sell more CDs.

While you're at the site, be sure to sign up for a free subscription to my e-mail newsletter, also called *The Buzz Factor*. The newsletter delivers a regular dose of music marketing tips and tools for songwriters, musicians and bands on a budget.

I'd love to hear from you, especially if you have a marketing tip or strategy you'd like to share with the nearly 10,000 music people who subscribe to *The Buzz Factor* newsletter.

Do yourself a favor and pay a visit to **TheBuzzFactor.com** the next time you're online. You'll be glad you did.

–Bob

Other books and resources by Bob Baker:

What Every Musician Should Know About Self-Promotion:
The 29 Key Principles of Independent Music Marketing

Music Marketing Crash Course: 1,001 Ways to Promote Yourself,
Make Money and Live Your Dreams

Unleash the Artist Within: Four Weeks to Transforming Your Creative
Talents Into More Recognition, More Profit and More Fun

Branding Yourself Online: How to Use the Internet
to Become a Celebrity or Expert in Your Field

E-zine Music Marketing: Powerful Ways to Promote Your Music
with a Fan E-mail Newsletter

Get more info at www.TheBuzzFactor.com